INSIGHT POCKET GUIDES

IRELAND

APA PUBLICATIONS

Dear Visitor!

Ireland is known for its bewitching scenery – woody dells, sombre bogs and sandy, shell-strewn coves. It is also famous for the charms of Dublin, for the Abbey Theatre, good pubs and a rich literary tradition. But as one of its best-known native sons, George Bernard Shaw, pointed out, Ireland is not simply a place, but rather a state of mind; it is romantic, passionate, garrulous. Here a stranger fast becomes a friend thanks to one of the chief pleasures of the Irish, conversation.

In these pages Insight Guides' correspondent in Ireland, Guy Mansell, has devised a series of 17 itineraries to help you experience the best of the emerald isle. He caters to a variety of time frames and tastes, from exploring the Guinness brewery in Dublin to sampling golden beaches and landscapes immortalised by W B Yeats and visiting abbeys and megalithic sites. He includes recommendations on where to stay en route, and abundant tips on restaurants.

Guy Mansell was delighted to write this Pocket Guide. It was, he says, an opportunity to share one of his enduring passions with people who, by the very act of choosing to come here, were likely to love the Irish landscapes and delight in its rich oral, literary and musical traditions. He offers his readers one piece of advice: 'Do not think you have to complete all of these itineraries and thus make a mad dash across the land under the ayatollah of clock time. Relax, reflect and remember that, in the words of the wise old proverb, 'there is as much to see in a blade of grass as in the whole meadow'.

Hans Höfer
Publisher, Insight Guides

CONTENTS

History & Culture
The arrival of the Celts, the invasion of the Normans, the Battle of the Boyne and the road to independence – a brief account of major events in Ireland's history............**10**

Ireland's Highlights
These itineraries concentrate on the highlights of Ireland. They are divided into six areas: Dublin and surroundings, the northwest, the far west, the mid-west, the southwest and the southeast. Each one is followed by a list of recommended hotels and restaurants.

Dublin
1 A Day in Dublin is a leisurely introduction to the city. Highlights include *Trinity College Library* and the *Book of Kells*, the *National Gallery of Ireland*, *St Patrick's Cathedral*, *Dublin Castle* and a flea market............**21**

2 The Boyne Valley is a circular day trip from Dublin. As well as the site of the Battle of the Boyne, it includes the megalithic graves of *Newgrange* and the *Hill of Slane* where St Patrick introduced Christianity **29**

3 Scenic County Wicklow explores the coast south of Dublin, from the *Joyce Museum* at *Sandycove* to *Russborough House*........................**32**

The Northwest
4 Donegal to Sligo is a leisurely day's drive, taking in *Donegal Abbey*, *Lisdall House*, *Drumcliffe* and the grave of W B Yeats with beaches en route **35**

5 Around Sligo – Yeats Country begins in *Sligo Town*, at the *Dominican Abbey* and museum, then heads out to *Rosses Point* and *Hazelwood*............**39**

The Far West
6 Westport comprises a tour of *Westport*, a drive along the shore of *Clew Bay* to the holy site of *Croagh Patrick* and an excursion to *Newport* and *Achill Island*..........**42**

7 Connemara is a circular drive from *Galway*, passing through some of the loveliest scenery in Ireland, including the *Connemara National Park* **46**

8 The Burren takes you from Galway to *Limerick*, stopping at *Dungaire Castle*, *Aillwee Caves*, *Leamanech Castle*, *Kilfenora* and *Lisdoonvarna*..................**51**

9 Limerick Interlude visits some of *Limerick's* 'theme attractions', in particular the *Craggaunowen* project at *Quin* and the castle at *Bunratty* **56**

10 Limerick to Tralee is a journey south, visiting the lovely village of *Adare*, *Matrix Castle*, *Ardagh*, *Foynes* and *Castleisland* with the *Crag Cave system*............**57**

Pages 2/3: West coast vista near Caherdaniel

11 The Dingle Peninsula explores one of the most beautiful areas in Ireland, where some 2,000 sites of antiquity have been identified...................**60**

The Southwest
12 Killarney to Bantry begins in *Killarney*, then goes to *Killarney National Park* and *Muckross Estates* and *Abbey*, burial site of some of Ireland's greatest poets, and up to *Torc Waterfall*...........................**63**

13 From Bantry to Kinsale starts with a scenic journey around the *Sheep's Head Peninsula*, heads for *Skibbereen* and *Baltimore*, then takes the coastal road to *Kinsale* via *Timoleague Abbey*..........................**66**

14 Kinsale and County Cork begins in *Kinsale* and proceeds to *Blarney Castle*, to kiss the famous stone, then on to the *Fota Estate Wildlife Park*.......**68**

The Southeast
15 Cork to Waterford is a day's drive, taking in *Mallow*, the *Blackwater Valley*, the gardens of *Anne's Grove*, *Fermoy*, *Lismore* and the seaport of *Youghal*.............**72**

16 Cashel and Kilkenny, a circular day-tour, takes you from *Waterford* to the religious complex of the *Rock of Cashel* and the medieval town of *Kilkenny*..........**75**

17 Waterford to Wexford takes in the crystal factory at *Kilbarry*, the *John F Kennedy National Park*, the fishing harbour at *Slade*, *Johnstone Castle* and the *Irish National Heritage Park*............................**78**

Shopping, Dining & Nightlife
What to buy, what to eat and where to stay up late..........**82–90**

Calendar of Events
A list of all the main events in an Irish year......................**91–2**

Practical Information
Essential background information, from climate to customs and transport to telecommunications.................**93–8**

Maps
Ireland and Great Britain.....4	*The Mid West I* 51
Ireland...........................18–19	*The Mid West II* 58
Dublin..................................22	*The Southwest* 63
Dublin and environs 29	*The Southeast I* 72
The Northwest....................35	*The Southeast II*.................75
The Far West......................42	

Index and Credits 106–12

Pages 8/9: Cashel Abbey

HISTORY & CULTURE

The Land of the Celts

Antiquities and unusual ruins of ancient monuments litter our itineraries as we travel across Ireland which incite curiosity. This small island contains some 130,000 monuments and, with aerial surveying, the count is increasing all the time.

The first signs of man in Ireland date from the Mesolithic era, some 8,000 years ago. Ireland was never under the auspices of the Roman Empire and the remains of her early peoples were left alone. Today this attracts archaeologists from all over the world to visit, dig and study. What little is known scholars have inferred from the ways in which the dead were buried and the artefacts found in tombs. There is nothing in Ireland as grand as the pyramids of the ancient pharaohs, although the huge burial mounds at Newgrange, Knowth and Dowth must have been awesome to behold in 2500BC.

We have a fuller picture of the Irish from the time of the Celts, themselves wandering arrivals from Europe who came to Ireland in the 6th century BC, although some scholars now say they arrived as far back as the 9th. Historians describe them as individualistic peoples who belonged to loosely knit communities with little political cohesion. Under Celtic rule, Ireland was divided into some 150 kingdoms, which gradually began to cement into larger groupings under the High Kings of Ulster, Connacht, Munster and Leinster.

Religion Old and New

After the fall of the Roman Empire, scholarly monks retreated westwards from those parts of northern Europe most ravaged by opportunistic invaders who picked on monasteries as easy prey. Refugee monks in the 5th century sought sanctuary in Ireland and kept Christian civilisation alive with their building, writing and teaching skills. There must have been agreement between Celts and Christians, as the old pagan sites served as the foundations for the new religion and for the construction of monastic settlements. There is

The organ in St Michan's Church

also evidence of harmony between Christian myth and the earlier Celtic pantheon of demi-gods, half-mortals and wizards, whose ancient lore was written down and not damned. These manuscripts of myths and legends are a valuable part of the nation's literary heritage. The most renowned is the mythological saga of *Tain Bo Cuailgne*, which now resides alongside the famous illuminated manuscript of the New Testament, known as the *Book of Kells*, in Trinity College Library, Dublin.

By the 7th and 8th centuries, Irish monasteries were renowned throughout Christendom for their Latin learning, writing and art. Pupils came to Ireland from the Continent, and staunch missionaries went out from Ireland with their message and teachings. This was the time of Ireland's Golden Age, when numerous monasteries were built with their churches, high crosses and round towers (which acted as beacons, bell towers and forts in time of siege). This was also the time when priceless art and bejewelled and enamelled artefacts were being made and manuscripts illuminated, like the *Book of Kells* (8th century), the Tara Brooch and the Ardagh Chalice (the latter two are now in the National Museum, Dublin).

By the end of the 8th century, the now thriving monasteries attracted pillaging and plundering from the Vikings, who established their settlements along Ireland's coast and founded ports such as Dublin, Wexford and Cork. Constant warfare between the invaders and the Celts finally resulted in the defeat of the Vikings by Brian Boru in 1014 at the Battle of Clontarf. Even so, Brian Boru, the most celebrated of Ireland's High Kings, died in the battle, and with his passing the old Gaelic order changed. For a century more, battles and turmoil prevailed until one king sought an alliance with the Normans in Wales, who only a hundred years before had invaded and subdued England successfully.

With the arrival of the Norman invaders led by Strongbow in 1169, came a new order; towns, ports, roads, laws and feudalism were established. The Normans suppressed the Celtic heritage but, being of the same faith, they vigorously

Donegal Castle

Head of the House

set about building bigger and better cathedrals, churches, abbeys, friaries, and priories which all reflected their advanced techniques. These again we will see on our travels, whether it be the grandiose religious complexes of Kilkenny and Kells or a simple Romanesque church on the Dingle Peninsula. Likewise castles mushroomed; the square Norman towers that we spy strewn across the landscape today were built, ravaged and rebuilt between the 13th and the 17th centuries.

The result of all this building is a palimpsest of history. As we travel round Ireland, it is not unusual to see a modern family home built against a broken castle of the 15th century, adjacent to a ruined monastic site of the 10th century with a 4,000-year-old cairn nearby. The events of ensuing centuries have left less of a mark on the landscape and impinge upon us little as we travel through the country, but they have left an indelible memory in the hearts and minds of the Irish people.

English Rule

With the Norman invasion, Ireland effectively came under the control of the English monarchs. Initially the incoming Normans intermarried, built their castles and extended their own influence to become powerful barons and landowners. It would not be long before an English monarch sought to exercise authority over these powerful and independent barons. Henry VIII demanded that all Irish lands be surrendered to him. Those who accepted Henry's dictum had their lands 'regranted by the grace of the King'. Those who refused had their lands taken away and given to the 'planters', loyal Protestant supporters of the king, many of them from England and Scotland.

The arrival of the planters sowed the seeds of the inter-religious strife that still divides Ulster today. Subsequently English monarchs pursued a policy of suppressing the Irish Catho-

A carved High Cross

lics, and Oliver Cromwell was one of the most ruthless of all: Irish rebellions were bloodily crushed by Cromwell's army between 1649 and 1652, after which most Irish lands that still remained in Catholic hands were granted to the Protestants. Matters came to a head in 1690 when the deposed Catholic King, James II of England, was defeated by William of Orange at the Battle of the Boyne, which took place near Dublin (see Itinerary 2). The following year, under the terms of the Treaty of Limerick, some 14,000 Irish soldiers and landowners were forced into exile, an event known ever since as the 'Flight of the Wild Geese'.

Ireland was left bereft of its young men and its leaders; new laws ensured that Catholics could only lease land for a maximum of 31 years. Resentment against absentee English landlords fanned the smouldering embers of Irish nationalism, but the road to independence was long, slow and bloody.

Despite the inequity and strife of the 18th century, it was a time of great building in Ireland, when the Georgian edifices that grace the centres of so many Irish cities were constructed. In Dublin, major public buildings rose on the banks of the River Liffey – the Bank of Ireland building (then the Irish Parliament), Leinster House and the Four Courts. With them came wide streets, crescents, squares and parks; mansions and terraced town houses. In the countryside palatial private residences, such as Russborough, Powerscourt, Castletown, Bantry and Newbridge House, to name but a few, were also being built by master architects.

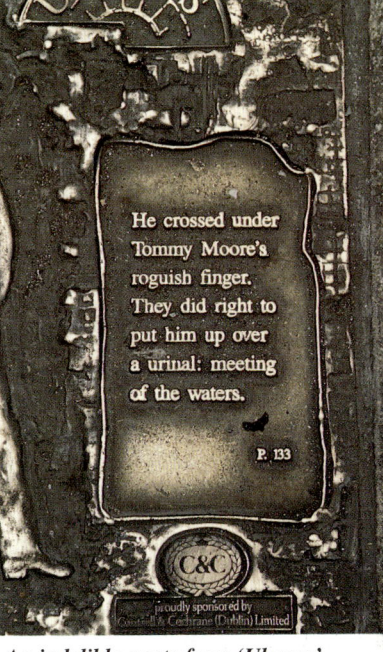

An indelible quote from 'Ulysses'

The Road to Independence

On the political front, the road to independence was marked by steps forward then backward. The Great Rebellion of 1798 against English rule, led by Wolfe Tone, was crushed with the loss of 50,000 lives. In 1800 the Irish parliament was dissolved and, under the Act of Union, Ireland became part of the United Kingdom, but without Catholic representation in the House of Commons; that did not come until 1829, with the passing of the Catholic Emancipation Act.

In 1845, potato blight destroyed crops of Ireland's staple food. The Great Famine hit the rural peasant hardest. It is said that a million people died of starvation and another million – driven off the land they could not afford to rent – emigrated to America. American Irish were later to provide the funds that supported the rising Republican movement, committed to achieving independence, even by armed struggle if necessary. Others sought effective but peaceful means to ensure that the Irish could own and farm their land. Charles Stewart Parnell set up the National Land League; supporters of the League agreed not to rent land from which the previous tenant had been evicted. Captain Boycott, who took over an estate in County Mayo, was so effectively ostracised by his neighbours that his name entered the language.

Parnell's objectives were relatively modest in that he sought 'Home Rule' for Ireland, rather than absolute independence. Ireland itself was divided and, whilst huge numbers of Irish volunteers were fighting for the British army on the Western Front during World War I, others joined the vigilante Irish Volunteers and staged the Easter Rising of 24 April 1916. The Volunteers occupied Dublin's General Post Office building for about a week before the British defeated them; all the leaders were executed and many of the participants were interned.

Independence finally came with the realisation that Britain could not force its rule on an unwilling population. Between 1919 and 1921, Britain and Ireland were effectively at war, with the Irish Republican Army pitted against British police and troops in an escalating spiral of violence and revenge killings. In October 1921, British and Irish representatives sat down in London to thrash out a settlement and the official independence document was finally signed on 5 December. That did not mean an end to Ireland's troubles, however. Civil war tore the country in 1922–3 over the issue of whether the government should accept the partition of Ireland – with the six counties of Ulster remaining part of the United Kingdom – or hold out for a united and independent Ireland.

The Republic Today

Today, the Republic of Ireland's two main political parties are the descendants of the civil war opponents: Fine Gael (who accepted partition) and Fianna Fáil (against partition). The problem of a divided Ireland has not gone away, but the Republic has matured to play an important part in the European Union and relations between Britain and Ireland – on the non-political level – are now stronger than they have ever been, especially since the United Kingdom is Ireland's main trading partner. Since entry to the EC in 1973, Ireland has profited

from European subsidies galore. European Structural Funds have been used to build new motorways, cultural centres and restore historic buildings, such as those in the Temple Bar quarter of Dublin. In 1994 increasing Irish prosperity meant that the Republic became ineligible for further large-scale subsidies, a source of mixed emotion there.

Economically, Ireland has traditionally been a farming country rather than an industrial manufacturer. For that reason, the rural way of life and the beauty of the countryside have survived as reminders of the way many other parts of developed Europe used to be. Some would say that Ireland is backward in that respect, but in fact, the unspoiled rivers and lakes with their ample stock of fish, Ireland's heritage of ancient monuments, the traditional music, the tinkers, horsedealers and donkey carts are now proving to be one of Ireland's major assets.

As more and more visitors discover this land that is relatively unspoiled by modernity, tourism is becoming one of the country's most important sources of revenue.

The growth of tourism has prompted the authorities to exploit natural sites and historic centres. One noticeable effect is the proliferation of controversial 'interpretative centres'. If sited beside a magnificent landscape, such as the Burren, they risk destroying the essence of the place but, if sensitively sited, they add to the visitors'

Monument in Dublin to Charles Stewart Parnell

Croagh Patrick, the holy mountain

appreciation. The best of these centres include the Famine Museum at Strokestown, which traces a poignant episode of Irish history, and the Queenstown Story at Cobh (*Itinerary 14*), which illuminates the history of Irish emigration. However, there is enough of genuine Irish heritage to celebrate without recourse to glossy packaging. Irish vernacular architecture is often underrated but is, in fact, surprisingly varied. Apart from the archetypal white thatched cottage (fast becoming extinct), neat slate-roofed cottages are equally traditional. The early Christian monastic sites, such as Glendalough (*Itinerary 3*) look quintessentially Irish; a lone round tower, several Celtic High Crosses and a couple of Romanesque chapels (often called 'tempealls' or temples) are commonplace.

On a grander scale, tower houses, fortified medieval structures, litter the landscape, matched by imposing castles at Kilkenny (*Itinerary 16*) and Limerick (*Itinerary 10*). In the archaeological field, Ireland has much to offer, from cairns to stone circles and enigmatic burial sites. Newgrange (*Itinerary 2*) is the greatest neolithic (late Stone Age) site but Sligo (*Itinerary 5*) is also rich in remains such as cairns. Lough Erne (*Itinerary 10*) is an excavated neolithic site, 15 dotted with stone circles, while Craggaunowen (*Itinerary 9*) incorporates authentic and reconstructed early Celtic architecture in a successful theme park. The Dingle Peninsula (*Itinerary 11*) is a unique Irish experience of Celtic antiquities and stupendous coastal scenery.

Historical Highlights

6,000BC First known traces of man in Ireland.
6th century Celtic migrations to Ireland.
AD432 St Patrick comes to Ireland as a missionary.
500–800 Early monasticism; Ireland is by now a major European centre of learning.
9th century Viking invasion and settlement.
841 Dublin is founded.
1014 Brian Boru defeats the Vikings and breaks their power.
1169 Norman invasion.
1537 Reformation doctrines promulgated by Henry VIII who orders the dissolution of the Irish monasteries.
1556 First 'planters' arrive from England and Scotland.
1649–52 The Great Rebellion is crushed by Cromwell.
1690 Battle of the Boyne.
1691 Treaty of Limerick and exile of the 'Wild Geese'.
1713 Jonathan Swift is appointed Dean of St Patrick's Cathedral in Dublin.
1798 Crushing of the second 'Great Rebellion', led by Wolfe Tone; 50,000 people die.
1800 The Act of Union.
1801 Legislative union of Great Britain and Ireland.
1829 Daniel O'Connell wins the right for Catholics to enter the British parliament.
1845 Beginning of the Great Famine caused by potato blight.
1858 Founding of the Irish Republican Brotherhood, forerunner of the IRA.
1875 Parnell is elected MP for Meath and becomes leader of the Home Rule movement.
1885 Parnell's party holds the balance of power in the House of Commons. Home Rule becomes a major issue but is defeated in the House of Lords.
1912 Protestants under Sir Edward Carson establish an illegal militia – the Ulster Volunteer Force – to oppose Home Rule; the south responds with the Irish National Volunteers.
1916 The Easter Rising leads to defeat for the Irish rebels, execution of their leaders, internment and imposition of martial law.
1918 Imprisoned Republicans go on hunger strike and the militant Sinn Fein party gains sweeping victories in the first post-war general election. Sinn Fein boycotts the House of Commons, sets up its own parliament in Ireland and elects the jailed Eamonn de Valera as president.
1919 Guerilla war between the IRA and British anti-terrorist forces – the 'Black and Tans'.
1921 Britain and Ireland sign a treaty granting Dominion status to most of Ireland. The six counties of Ulster remain part of the United Kingdom.
1922–3 Civil war between pro- and anti-partitionists in Ireland
1939–45 Controversially, Ireland remains neutral in World War II.
1949 Ireland becomes a Republic.
1969 Outbreak of 'the troubles' in Northern Ireland.
1973 Ireland joins the European Community (now the EU).
1988 Dublin celebrates its 'millennium' – 147 years late.
1993-4 The Downing Street Agreement between the Dublin and London governments started a new peace dialogue culminating in an IRA ceasefire and a tentative end to 'the armed struggle.'
1994 The European elections confirm the political status quo in the Republic.

Day Itineraries

Ireland is the most westerly country in Europe. Politically, the island nation is divided into the Republic of Ireland, which became independent in 1921, and six counties of Ulster – known as Northern Ireland – which remain part of the United Kingdom. This guide covers the Republic and in particular the coastal counties, the most rewarding to visitors.

The first three itineraries are based in Dublin, Ireland's capital. The remaining 14 itineraries are organised geographically, starting in the north in Donegal, working southward to Bantry and then eastward from Cork to Wexford. The itineraries assume that you will hire a car and drive around Ireland.

Since each of the itineraries lasts a full day, it would be impossible to follow all of them in the course of a short visit. The aim is that you should choose and combine those itineraries that most interest you. Most are accessible from Dublin.

If you are a lover of remote scenic beauty, then you will probably find *Itineraries 4–8* of particular interest, whilst *Itineraries 9–17* cover that part of Ireland that has most by way of castles, manors, monuments and museums.

The dramatic Ring of Kerry

1. A Day in Dublin

Your first day in Ireland is best spent getting to know the capital and the best way to do this is on foot. Dublin is one of Europe's smallest capital cities and all the important sights are within walking distance. This leisurely day-long itinerary will help you soak up the atmosphere of this characterful city and show you the major sights: Trinity College Library and the *Book of Kells*; the National Gallery of Ireland; Dublin Castle; Christchurch Cathedral; Dublinia; the Guinness Brewery and Temple Bar.

Leave your car safely locked in the hotel car park for the day (as in all European capitals, finding secure street parking is difficult at the best of times). Walk or take a taxi to the **Thomas Davis Theatre**, Trinity College Library to see the audio-visual presentation, *The Dublin Experience* (daily, late May to September; 10am–5pm). This will help you orientate yourself and learn something of the city's history.

Founded by Vikings in AD841, the walled town of Dublin hardly grew during the Middle Ages when the principal public buildings were its castle, of which the Record Tower is original, and Christchurch Cathedral. By the 17th century the city was in virtual decay, but flourished suddenly in the 18th century with a sensational building programme to which Dublin's fine looks are attributed. But with the termination of legislative independence from England in 1801, Dublin's upper crust faded away and a decline set in. With the famine and land clearances that followed throughout the 19th century, the displaced came to Dublin and many a fine street descended to slum. Only through political and

Trinity College, Dublin

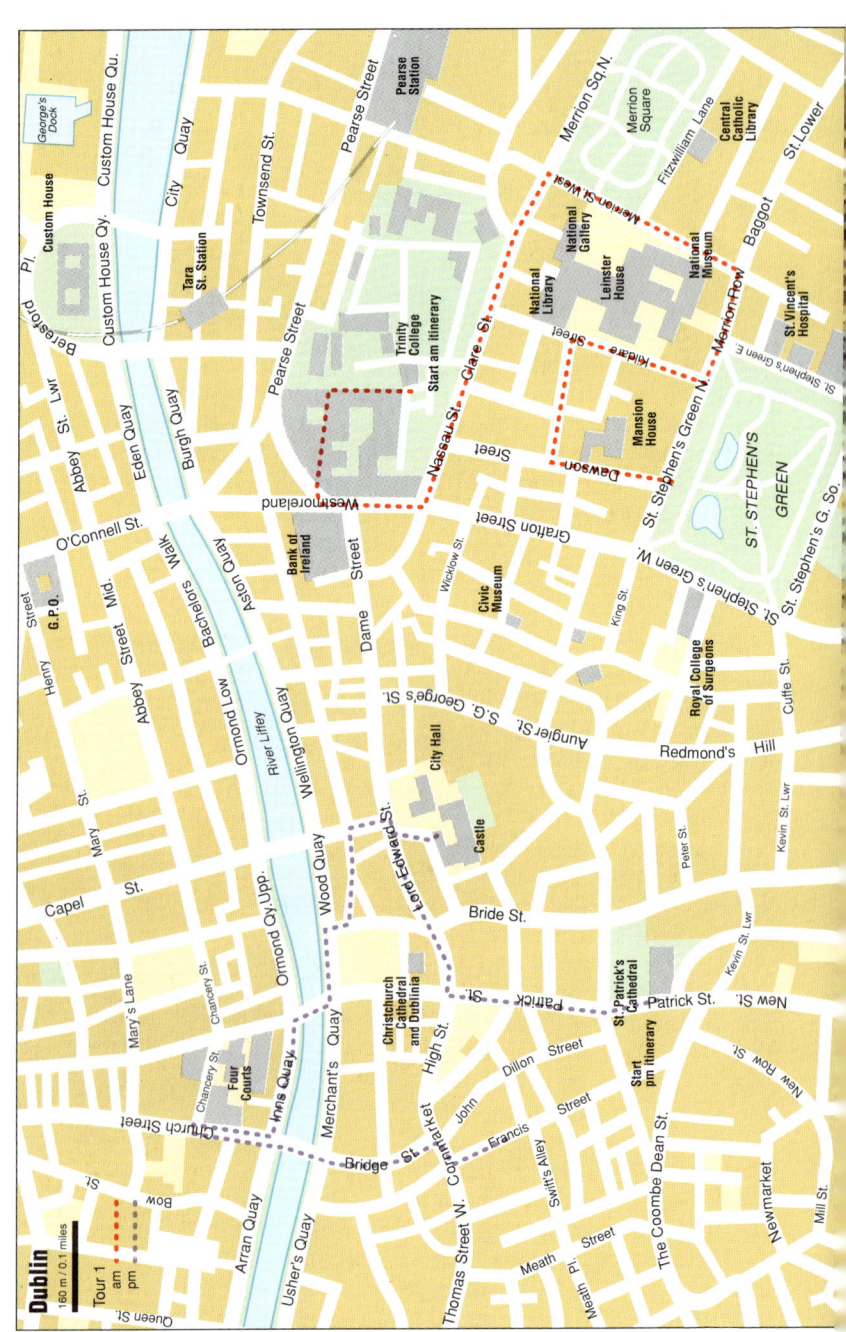

The Bank of Ireland

social revolution, since independence, has Dublin been able to restore its splendid Georgian architecture.

We will see some of Dublin's Georgian crescents and squares later in the day. For now, having viewed the audio-visual presentation, move on to Trinity College Library's **Long Room** (Monday to Saturday, 9.30am–4.30pm; Sunday, noon–5pm). This houses some 200,000 books and manuscripts, the highlight being the 8th-century illuminated *Book of Kells*. Other national treasures are also on view, including the Brian Boru harp. On leaving the library, take the exit to the University. Cross the cobbled way and go out via the main entrance onto **College Green**, flanked by statues of two of its alumni, the orator **Edmund Burke** and dramatist **Oliver Goldsmith**. In front is the distinctive **Bank of Ireland** building, built in 1729 to house the Irish parliament but made redundant after parliament voted itself out of existence when authority was transferred to London in 1801. Visitors are welcome (weekdays, 10am–4pm), but guided tours are only given on Tuesday.

From here turn around and retrace your steps past the college up Westmoreland Street. On the right-hand side is the statue of **Molly Malone**. Love it or hate it, this busty statue is a great favourite with visitors to the city, many of whom cannot help bursting into a rendition of 'Cockles and mussels, alive, alive O!' Tempted as you may be to continue up the pedestrian way of Grafton Street, I recommend going left along **Nassau** Street which continues as Leinster Street. This is something of a centre for craft shops, chief amongst which are Blarney Woollen Mills and the Kilkenny Shop. At the end of Leinster Street, turn right at Merrion Street Upper, just after Green's famous book store, well worth a browse. Across the road is **Merrion Square**, one of Dublin's finest addresses. The first turn on the right takes us up to the **National Gallery of Ireland** (Monday to Saturday, 10am–6pm; Thursday, 10am–9pm; Sunday, 2–5pm). It is worth visiting the newly-refurbished gallery to see the Rembrandts, a recently discovered Caravaggio and an underrated but distinguished Anglo-Irish collection. Fitzer's restaurant inside is a great place for coffee or an early lunch.

Continuing up Merrion Street we pass **Leinster House**, built in 1745,

A Georgian door

The Ardagh Chalice

and now the seat of the Irish parliament. Down at the end of the wrought-iron palings is the **Natural History Museum** which has an extensive collection Despite its local nickname as the 'Dead Zoo', the museum houses a weird yet endearing collection. Next we turn right on Merrion Row, getting our first glimpse of the magnificent buildings around St Stephen's Green. Just past the Shelbourne Hotel, where the Constitution was drawn up, is Kildare Street into which we turn. Do visit the **National Museum** (Tuesday to Saturday, 10am–5pm; Sunday, 2–5pm) with its unique collection of archaeological artefacts. Amongst these are the **Ardagh Chalice**, the Cross of Cong and the Tara Brooch, all superb examples of Celtic craftsmanship.

Next door is the main entrance to Leinster House. We cross over the road, turn left along Molesworth Street and left again up Dawson Street. Immediately on the left is **St Anne's Church**, noted for its lunch-time recitals (weekdays, 10am–3pm). We then pass the **Royal Irish Academy Library** with its collection of manuscripts (weekdays, 9.30am–5.30pm), then the Lord Mayor's residence known as the Mansion House (1710).

Facing us is **St Stephen's Green**, claimed to be Europe's largest square. This large expanse of landscaped gardens was a Common until 1664. By Georgian times, the Green was an elegant spot, lined by gracious 18th-century mansions, many of which remain. The neat flowerbeds and ponds in the park were financed by the Guinness brewing dynasty in the 1880s.

Now is a good time to be thinking of lunch. Shops around Grafton Street, off the northwest corner of the Green, will supply you with all the ingredients for a picnic which you can share with the ducks in St Stephen's Green park. Alternatively, the Green has several restaurants, from the formality of the Shelbourne Hotel dining rooms to the elegance of the Commons Restaurant (Newman House, 85 St Stephen's Green; Tel: 4780530) This erstwhile seat of University College Dublin, in addition to reasonable food, boasts a superb palladian plasterwork, as befits the finest Georgian interior in Dublin.

After lunch take a taxi to **St Patrick's Cathedral** (daily in summer, 9am–6pm; winter, 9.30am–12.30pm and 1.30–6pm), believed to be founded on the site where St Patrick baptised converts. There are many monuments here to ponder over, including the bust and epitaph of Jonathan Swift

24

Detail from Dublin Castle

(notable author of *Gulliver's Travels*), who was dean here for 30 years. Look out, too, for the Chapter House door, with its hole, from which the expression 'chancing your arm' was derived.

From here we head towards the River Liffey, along Patrick Street, to **Christchurch Cathedral** (daily in summer, 10am–5pm; in winter closed between 1pm and 2pm daily); this was founded in 1038 although the current structure dates to the late 12th century, as the cathedral took over a century and a half to build. If you have the energy, first visit **Dublinia** (daily, 10am–5pm), set in Synod Hall, next door to the cathedral. This multi-media exhibition brings to life medieval Dublin and displays reconstructions of old buildings. A bridge links the exhibition with the cathedral, and a tour of the building is included in the entrance fee. Don't miss the effigy of a recumbent knight with a small figure lying alongside. Legend has it that this is the **tomb of Strongbow**, the knight who conquered Ireland for the Normans. Some say the smaller figure is Eva, his wife, and others that it is Strongbow's son – the youth is supposed to have fled from the battlefield and Strongbow punished his cowardice by executing him.

Turning from such gruesome thoughts, walk down Lord Edward Street to **Dublin Castle** (weekdays, 10am–12.15pm and 2–5pm; weekends, 2–5pm). The castle dates from 1204, but only the Record Tower survives from Norman times. Acting as the administrative centre of English power, the castle was subject to attack and was badly damaged by a fire in 1684 and the events of the 1916 Easter Rising. The present castle is a palatial affair but it is worth visiting the grim undercroft which contains elements of the original Viking and Norman strongholds. The main feature is a lavish set of State Apartments, surrounding a magnificent courtyard, designed as ceremonial quarters for the English Viceroys who once ruled

St Patrick's Cathedral, Dublin

Ireland. Also worth noting is the statuary on the walls – 90 carved heads of British monarchs and bishops.

From the castle, go down to **Wood Quay**, on the banks of the Liffey; it was here that the Vikings founded the first city of Dublin in the 9th century. Office blocks now stand over the archaeological site where the Viking remains were found. Cross the Liffey to reach the **Four Courts** on the opposite bank. This great classical building, dominating the Northern Quays, was completed in the late 18th century and is the home of the Irish Law Courts. Although it was partly destroyed in the 1922 Civil War its restoration has been much admired. Equally fascinating are the rascally looking characters waiting to enter the courts with their bewigged lawyers, to answer the call of justice.

Leaving the Four Courts, we turn right on Church Street to visit the church of **St Michan** dating from the 17th century. The organ, upon which Handel is said to have played, features some excellent wood carvings. The church's other major curiosity is the vault where bodies have lain for centuries without decomposing and are now completely mummified. From here, we turn around and wander across the bridge and along Bridge Street, past the Brazen Head Hotel. After turning right on Cornmarket, look for Francis Street, the main street for antique shops, second left across the road. A few yards down is the entrance to Dublin's most colourful **flea market**, founded by Lord Iveagh for itinerant street vendors in 1907. The carved stone head above the portal, with its 'smoking cap', is thought to be the market's benefactor. By now you have earned a rest, so take a taxi back to the elegant bars of the Shelbourne Hotel.

If young and energetic, instead explore Dublin's bohemian 'Left Bank', called Temple Bar. To get there, stroll down Lord Edward Street, past Dublin Castle, and take any turning left off Dame Street. Plan your evening while drinking a Guinness in the art deco downstairs bar of the Clarence Hotel (Wellington Quay), owned by the rock band U2. This is the heart of **Temple Bar,** a vibrant and slightly bohemian quarter which dates back to the 18th century. Then it was a raffish, low-life quarter but, after surviving demolition in the 1960s, it is now the 'alternative' cultural centre, set amongst tiny alleys between Dane Street and the quayside. There is a variety of trendy bars and restaurants but you may prefer a literary pub crawl (starting 7.30pm nightly at the Bailey, Duke Street, in summer).

Tomorrow we will be heading northward out of town to explore the Boyne Valley – unless you are so enamoured of Dublin's charm that you want to spend another day in the city. If so, I suggest you spend the day shopping (see *Shopping* section) and consider a visit to the **Guinness Brewery** (8 Crane Street) whence the dark stout has been flowing for 230 years. It is open from 10am–4.30pm Monday to Friday and the visitor centre, known as the **Hop Store**, offers an excellent audio-visual presentation and various items of brewing memorabilia – and a tasting!

Dublin is known for its fresh produce

Restaurants

For Dubliners, dining in a restaurant is an occasion; the design and décor of the surroundings, the clientele and the whole atmosphere are equally as important as the food. In this small city, restaurants tend to be distinctive. As in most capitals, the top of the market is dominated by the French interpretations, but in Dublin all cuisine has its own special character due to the freshness and purity of the ingredients available here. Fish is landed and eaten on the same day. The very quality of all the 'raw' foods presents a persistent incentive and challenge to chefs. This has helped stamp a distinctively Irish culinary individuality – even 'sushi' is Irish, when it is sliced from a locally caught salmon! Dublin now offers such cosmopolitan cuisine as Pacific Rim and Provençale, Chinese and cajun, with American and Italian influences predominating.

The ratings in this guide refer to a meal for two with wine:
$$$ = Expensive (over £50)
$$ = Moderate (£30–£50)
$ = Inexpensive (under £30)

RESTAURANT PATRICK GUILBAUD
46 James Place, Dublin 2
Tel: 01-6764192. $$$
Dublin's most serious, most formal French restaurant with a Michelin one star rating. The highly professional, innovative kitchen is known for turning the finest of Ireland's 'freshest' into art. Their gastronomic Menu Surprise of six courses is created individually for each order.

L'ECRIVAIN
112 Baggot Street Lower, Dublin 2
Tel: 01-6611919. $$$
The theme of this small basement restaurant is literary Dublin. The walls are hung with portraits of great writers, whilst bookshelves are casually stacked with well-thumbed volumes. Classically cooked game is especially good, from a very highly competent kitchen. Excellent service.

GALLAGHERS BOXTY HOUSE
20 Temple Bar, Dublin 2
Tel: 01-6772762. $/$$
This restaurant centres its menu around Ireland's traditional food: 'boxty' is a potato pancake packed

with lots of different fillings. The rest of the menu follows the 'home' theme with good versions of Irish stew, colcannon and bread and butter pudding. The ambience is 'cottagey', and the waiting area is the pub across the road.

TOSCA
20 Suffolk Street, Dublin
Tel: 01-6796744. $$
Run by U2 Bono's brother, this chic modern restaurant offers 'new' Mediterranean cuisine.

THE TEA ROOM
Clarence Hotel
Wellington Quay, Dublin
Tel: 01-6776178. $$
Eclectic cuisine (not tea!) in an art nouveau ballroom, from Pacific Rim to modern Italian.

CHEZ JULES
D'Olier Chambers
16A D'Olier Street, Dublin
Tel: 01-6770499. $
A lively French bistro which has an Irish twist.

CHOMPYS
Powerscourt Townhouse, Dublin
Tel: 01-6794552. $
Jewish-American style deli with a great brunch or lunch often accompanied by live music in the courtyard.

Hotels

The art of innkeeping seems to come naturally to Dubliners. This city, one of the smallest European capitals, has a surprising number of luxury hotels.

THE BERKELEY COURT
Lansdowne Road, Dublin 4
Tel: 01-6601711. $$$
International-style hotel set and elegance in the Ballsbridge district.

THE CLARENCE
6-8 Wellington Quay
Dublin
Tel: 01-6776178. $$$
This stylish hotel, owned by the rock group U2, has art deco rooms and a lovely restaurant.

GEORGIAN HOUSE HOTEL
20 Lower Baggot Street, Dublin
Tel: 01-6618832. $
A charming, central period house.

KILRONAN HOUSE
70 Adelaide Road, Dublin 2
Tel: 01-4755266. $
Small, central, family-run guest house.

LANSDOWNE
27 Pembroke Road, Dublin 4
Tel: 01-6762549. $/$$
Friendly small hotel in the Ballsbridge district.

THE SHELBOURNE
St Stephen's Green, Dublin 2
Tel: 01-6766471. $$$
Ireland's most distinguished address; a grand hotel where the Constitution was drafted. The rooms may be a bit cramped but the elegant surroundings are compensation enough. Delightful but formal bars – great for afternoon tea or drinks.

TEMPLE BAR HOTEL
Temple Bar, Dublin
Tel: 01-6773333. $$
Cheerful hotel with good restaurants. Convenient for both Temple Bar and business quarter.

THE WESTBURY
Grafton Street, Dublin 2
Tel: 01-6791122. $$$
Modern international hotel well located in the shopping district – very convenient.

2. The Boyne Valley

This circular day trip takes us north of Dublin to the Boyne Valley where 5,000 years of history are encapsulated in the megalithic graves of Newgrange, the Hill of Slane where Christianity was brought to Ireland by St Patrick, monastic remains and aristocratic houses and the site of the Battle of the Boyne.

From Dublin city we follow the airport signs, which will take us northward on the N1. Passing by the airport, we continue on to Swords, where we turn right to Malahide on the R106, following the signs to **Malahide Castle** (weekdays, 10am–5pm; November to March weekends, 2–5pm; April to October weekends, 11am–6pm). This was founded in Norman times and for 800 years was the seat of the Talbot family. The castle is now owned by Dublin City, and houses the National Gallery's portrait collection, Ireland's largest. It is said that on the morning before the Battle of the Boyne, 14 of the family breakfasted together; none returned. Today the medieval Great Hall is used for state banquets. The outbuildings house the Cecil Fry model railway collection.

We retrace our route back along the R106 and turn right before Swords to continue north on the N1. Approximately 5km (3 miles) on, we turn right on the R127 to **Lusk**. St Mac Cuilinn, who died in 497, is buried in a cave here, though nobody is quite sure where. Most noticeable is the unusual conglomeration of towers, linking the ancient 'pencil' round tower to the church (built in 1500) with its three round structures on each corner. Back on the R127, a peaceful and quiet road across gentle farmlands, we continue to Skerries, said to be the spot where St Patrick landed to convert the Irish to Christianity in the 5th century. We carry on along the coast to Balbriggan, a fishing village, and on to **Drogheda**. This historic seaport began with the Vikings, became a Norman stronghold

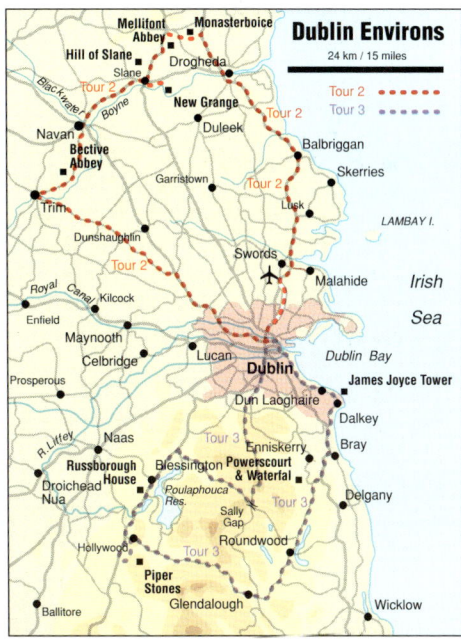

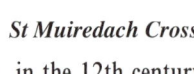

St Muiredach Cross

in the 12th century and truly flourished in the 15th century. In 1649 Cromwell's army committed an atrocious massacre here, burning defenders and civilians alive in St Peter's Church. The church is also famous for St Oliver Plunkett, executed in 1681, whose head lies embalmed on the far side of the altar. The town has many beautiful buildings and anyone who wants to linger can obtain details of walking tours from the tourist centre.

If you are here around lunchtime, you will not be disappointed by the **Sennhof Restaurant** at the Boyne Valley Hotel (Dublin Road, Drogheda; Tel: 041-37737) which serves authentic Swiss food.

Some 6km (3¾ miles) beyond Drogheda on the N1 we pick up the signs for the **Boyne Valley Trail** and begin the real part of this journey. Very shortly we arrive at **Monasterboice**, one of Ireland's exceptional monastic sites. The site dates from the rather obscure St Buite, who died in 521. The monastery fell into disuse in the 12th century and only ruins remain, except for the most excellent Round Tower and three high crosses. The finest of these is the St Muiredach Cross with its interlaced motifs and carvings; these are thought to depict scenes from the book of Genesis, including Adam and Eve, and Cain and Abel.

We continue to follow the trail signs to the huge Cistercian site of **Mellifont Abbey**, which finally fell into disuse in the 18th century; in the 13th century this was the ecclesiastical centre for some 35 other monasteries in the district. Of special interest is the octagonal *lavabo* (wash-room), with its Romanesque features. We continue on the trail southwest to the rather muddy looking River Boyne, with pleasant deciduous woods and fields along its banks, to the **battle site**. It was here, in 1690, that the forces of William of Orange defeated King James II, which lost him his claim to the British throne. As battles go, it was not especially bloody but it transformed English, French and Irish history. The battlefield is well signposted with a viewing point and an explanation of the manoeuvres and tactics of both forces.

We take up the signs again, this time to reach sensational **Newgrange** (October

to April daily, 10am–4.30pm; May to September daily, 9.30am–7pm). This massive 5,000-year-old passage grave, with its glistening white quartz walls surrounding some 200,000 tons of rock, has been thoroughly excavated. Similar tombs at **Knowth** and **Dowth** are still being worked over. Newgrange tomb is rated as one of the most spectacular archaeological sites in Europe. The excellent guided tour takes us 19m (62ft) into its central chamber decorated with the Neolithic ring markings. The highlight is the well-presented re-enactment of the tomb's astronomical significance; light floods the chamber to represent the beam of sunlight that penetrates the core for some 20 minutes at the winter solstice. Emerging from the tomb, one hardly notices that the hillside, hidden from view by hedges, is carved with humps, tumps and megaliths in their hundreds, indicating how impressive the area must have been around 3000BC.

Site of the Battle of the Boyne

Our next move takes us the short distance along a narrow lane to the neat and charming manorial village of **Slane**. At the west end is the castle seat of the Mountcharles family, now a venue for pop concerts but currently being restored after a devastating fire. The village is better known as the home of the soldier poet Francis Ledgwig. One kilometre (half a mile) north, on the N2, is the **Hill of Slane** where St Patrick lit a great bonfire for Christianity in AD433. This event is not chronicled at the site, which has interesting ecclesiastical ruins associated with St Earc. If you have not yet had lunch, the **Conygham Arms Hotel** (Tel: 041-24155) in the centre of Slane offers a hearty self-service buffet. Leaving Slane in a westerly direction our route now takes us to Navan on the N51, the county town of Meath, centre for furniture making and nearby lead and zinc mines. Our main target is **Bective Abbey**, some 8km (5 miles) beyond on the R161 Trim road. We could, of course, turn off for the Hill of Tara, celebrated in Irish song and legend, but most visitors find this a great disappointment with little to see. Bective Abbey has more to offer, even though the sense of legend might be less powerful. This delightful ruin of an abbey that was founded in the mid-12th century contains the body of Hugh de Lacy, who died in 1195, minus his head which was interred in

Newgrange tomb

Dublin. A 10-year dispute arose when the monks sought the return of the head, resulting in a ruling from the Pope in Avignon.

A further 8km (5 miles) takes us to **Trim**, dominated by its 12th-century D-shaped castle, regarded as a classic example of its type since it has undergone very little alteration since the day it was built. The town also offers an intriguing group of medieval monuments including the Yellow Steeple, built on the site of an Augustinian abbey that once housed a fabled statue of Our Lady, destroyed during the Reformation. Some 2km (1¼ miles) further on is the long church of Saints Peter and Paul; the refectory building creates a curious echo if you yell at it from the friary of St John the Baptist, across the river. Trim castle has a visitor centre that helps explain the town's medieval monuments. From here, Dublin is some 38km (23½ miles) southeast along the R154 and N3.

3. Scenic County Wicklow

A day-long drive south from Dublin, following the coast to the James Joyce Tower, through wooded valleys to Powerscourt House with its ornate gardens, and on to the historic ecclesiastical site of Glendalough, then Russborough House with its art treasures, before crossing the mountains at Sally Gap and returning to Dublin. This is a favourite getaway trail for Dubliners.

Drive south from Dublin along Merrion Road or Beach Street following the signs for Blackrock or Dun Laoghaire. At the seaside suburb of Sandycove is the **Joyce Museum** located in the old Martello tower that features in the opening scene of *Ulysses*. Various morsels of Joyce memorabilia are displayed, including manuscripts and musical instruments. Below the tower is Forty Foot, a deep bathing pool, where male nudity prevailed until recently.

The Wicklow Mountains

Powerscourt Waterfall

Beyond lies the appropriately named Sorrento Road following the cliff top; this flows into Vico Road, with its noble views of Killiney Bay and Dalkey Island. At the railway station turn right up Military Road, away from the coast, then left (south) on the N11. Turn off right when you see the sign for **Powerscourt** (daily, March to October, 9.30am–5.30pm). Although this Palladian mansion of 1740 is now a shell, following a disastrous fire, the formal gardens – embellished with statues, elegant wrought-iron work, and pebble-mosaic terraces – are fabled throughout Europe for their layout and setting. In addition there are Italian, Japanese and walled gardens, plus herbaceous borders and greenhouses, to be enjoyed. After a gentle stroll to the dramatic lake and sunken Japanese gardens, consider sinking into the cosy estate tea-rooms.

Our next stop, still within the estate, is the **Powerscourt Waterfall** (daily, 9.30am–7pm) with 90m (300ft) of silvery ribbon tumbling into a wooded glen, an ideal area for walks and picnics for much of the year, but perhaps a little too busy in high summer for real peace and quiet. Ahead lies **Glendalough** – the valley with the two lakes. Simply follow the signs along the R755. The Glendalough (Tel: 0404-45135) is a good place for lunch in a dining room that has splendid views of the monastic ruins. It is ironic that St Kevin, who gave up the good life to become a recluse, and who founded this enormous monastic settlement around AD570, should now be the top-of-the-tourist-pops. Glendalough (open daily, mid-October to mid-March 9.30am–5.30pm; 9.30am–6pm the rest of the year) is best explored by starting at the visitor centre, seeing the audio-visual presentation and enjoying the brilliant exhibition about Ireland's early ecclesiastical sites. The most accessible churches are the **Cathedral**, a Romanesque church containing early Christian gravestones, and **St Kevin's Kitchen**, the tiny, oddly-named church, topped by a small round tower. If you happen to be there when there are few visi-

Formal Powerscourt gardens

tors, you will feel a sense of serenity descend on the valley, encouraging you to wander amongst the sites scattered over a 2.5km (1½ mile) stretch of the valley. The centre's curator knows all there is to know about St Kevin and the legends which do not appear in any book.

From Glendalough continue west on the R756 to Hollywood. The idea is to turn right to Russborough House, but if addicted to stone circles then turn left for the **Piper Stones**, so called because legend has it that this is the place where the fairies gather to play the Irish bagpipes. Having visited the mysterious stones, turn around and drive northward up the N81, turning left at the sign for **Russborough House** (daily Easter to October, 10.30am–5.30pm; closed out of season. Tel: 045-65239.) This Palladian mansion, lying in wooded parkland, was built in 1750 for the Earl of Milltown Although the house has suffered from IRA-funded thefts of its art collection, and the finest paintings are now in Dublin's National Gallery, there is still much to see, from paintings to period furniture. Russborough is the most lavishly decorated and furnished mansion in the southeast. The grandest room is the saloon, with its feast of rococo plasterwork, attributed to the masterly Francis brothers. Equally fine is the exuberantly stuccoed staircase, swathed in hunting scenes

From here drive on to Blessington via the N81 and continue beside the man-made Blessington Lakes before turning right for **Sally Gap** a few kilometres beyond. This begins a spectacularly scenic drive across high uplands and along the remote ridges of the Wicklow Mountains, without a building in sight. At Sally Gap itself turn left; there is no sign but that is the direction for Dublin. Here we are close to the source of the River Liffey. You will notice the peat cutting areas in this upland bog to which Dubliners have ancient rights. Simply follow the road, which all too soon descends to the city.

Palladian Russborough House

The Northwest

4. Donegal to Sligo

You can drive from Donegal town to Sligo in an hour but we will take all day, beginning with a look at Donegal town, then taking in Lough Eske, the Creevykeel Court Cairn and, perhaps, a boat ride out to Innishmurray. Then we will visit Lissadell House and Drumcliffe, with its high cross and the churchyard where W B Yeats lies. On this drive you are never more than five minutes from golden beaches so, if the weather is good, plan for a swim and sunbathing.

Donegal town was founded by the Vikings at the point where the Eske River meets the sea. This is a delightful town with a centre known as the 'Diamond', where an obelisk celebrates the memory

Donegal town

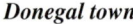

of Brother Michael O'Cleary's classic work, the *Annals of the Four Masters*. This was the first real history of Ireland, finished in 1636 and today considered a literary masterpiece.

The **castle** ruin beside the swift-running Eske was once the seat of the O'Donnells. The last of this ancient clan, Red Hugh O'Donnell, was forced into exile in 1607. The Jacobean ruin is attributed to Sir Basil Brooke, a planter, who transformed it into a residence in 1610 after the banishment of the last chief. Beside the estuary lie the remains of **Donegal Abbey**, founded in 1474 but wrecked by an enormous explosion during a military siege in 1601.

The town's most famous shop is the Magee department store (located on the Diamond) which stocks a range of handwoven tweeds. As well as selling ready-made clothing, Magee's has a working handloom, an exact replica of those still used in over a hundred Donegal homes to produce tweeds for this long-established company. Just 6km (3¾ miles) north of the town is Lough Eske backed by the Blue Stack Mountains.

Before setting off south, you might like to take the delightful drive around the lake on narrow wooded lanes. This detour will take just under an hour – unless you are tempted to stop at **Harvey's Point**, a formal country club with hotel and restaurant offering hill-walking, riding and char fishing in Lough Eske. For lunch sample the restaurant's Fisherman's Platter, or return to Donegal for St Ernan's House or the Hyland Hotel. In Donegal town, turn left at the Diamond onto the Sligo road, the N15. A kilometre out is the **Donegal Craft Village**, worth a few minutes' browse amongst the shops and studios making and selling pottery, ceramics, textiles, metalwork and jewellery.

Some 12km (7½ miles) further on we turn right to Rossnowlagh to take the R231, a quieter and more scenic route to **Ballyshannon**, with its magnificent 4km (2½ miles) of sandy beach. The ruins of Kilbarron Castle are to be found at the southern end, whilst Ballyshannon itself is dominated by a modern friary housing an historical museum. At the **Donegal Parian China factory**, just outside the town on the N15, you can tour the workshops any day from May to September. After lingering a while in Ballyshannon, with its steep and picturesque main street, we move on, looking across Donegal Bay with the might of the Slieve League in the far distance. Pass through Bundoran, a spreading seaside resort, and turn left after some 8km (5 miles) to the **Creevykeel Court Cairn**, one of the most extensive in Ireland. Finds from the 1935 Harvard University dig date the tomb to around 2500BC. It is believed that the unroofed courts at the entrances were used by worshippers or mourners.

On the opposite side of the N15 we shall take the R279, a 5km (3 mile) detour to **Mullaghmore** to see the harbour and admire its sandy beach. It is worth taking a boat trip to **Innishmurray Island** 7km (4¼ miles) off the Sligo coast. This well-preserved monastic site is surrounded by a stone cashel, or a defensive stone wall. Inside the walls you will find a collection of churches, beehive huts, cross-decorated slabs and the famous cursing stones, a relic of Ireland's pagan past.

Back on the N15 we turn south to Grange and start to feel the enchantment of **Benbulben**, the mountain that dominates the landscape on our left. If you are in no hurry, I do advise turning right and following the coastal roads, many of which are so little used that grass grows down the middle; the beaches beckon and there is the unique feeling of travelling between the masses of Benbulben and the Slieve League out across the water.

There are no signs to follow except near Raghly, where you should look for **Lissadell House** on the Lissadell estate (June to September, Monday to Saturday 10am–noon and 2–4pm).

Donegal Castle

This Victorian pile is the seat of the Gore-Booth family and is currently in terrible condition. It is difficult to understand why it has been allowed to become so neglected, having been the home of one Ireland's finest daughters, Constance Gore-Booth, Countess Markievicz, who was both a freedom fighter, and the first woman ever elected to Britain's House of Commons.

From Lissadell it is 5km (3 miles) to **Drumcliffe**, notable for the stump of an early Christian round tower, which was reduced by lightning to its present height in 1396. Legend says the rest will fall down when the wisest man on earth passes beneath. Opposite, in the churchyard amongst the trees, is the **grave of W B Yeats**. Beside the small car park is a fine sculptured high cross,

Donegal Craft Village

> Cast a cold Eye
> On Life, on Death.
> Horseman, pass by!
>
> W. B. YEATS
>
> June 13th 1865
> January 28th 1939

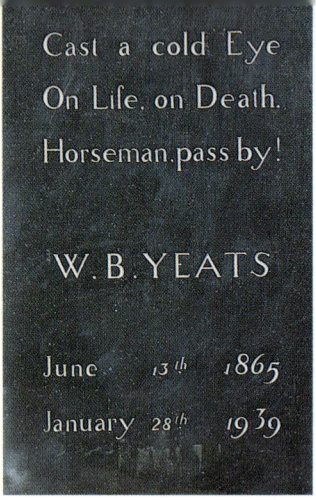

The poet's epitaph

carved with Old Testament scenes dating from the 10th century, all that remains of a monastery founded by St Colmcille in AD 575.

The grave of the Nobel Prize-winning poet lies to the left of the church. On the stone are inscribed the words: 'Cast a cold Eye / on Life, on Death. / Horseman, pass by!'

It was Yeats' wish to lie beneath Benbulben and the inscription is the coda of his epitaph: 'Under bare Ben Bulben's head, In Drumcliffe Churchyard Yeats is laid'. The poet died in France in 1939, leaving behind a body of work which is Irish literature at its finest. His remains were thrown into a French paupers' grave. How much of his body was interred here in 1948 is a moot point but even if only a bone, Benbulben guards Yeats' dream. Sligo is 8km (5 miles) south along the N15.

Hotels and Restaurants

Donegal

HARVEY'S POINT
Lough Eske, Donegal, Co Donegal
Tel: 073-22208. $$$
Reservations and jacket and tie advised for this high-quality restaurant serving French and Swiss cuisine.

HYLAND HOTEL
The Diamond, Donegal, Co Donegal
Tel: 073-21027. $$/$$$
In the centre of town and local social life. Rooms overlooking the bay.

ST ERNAN'S HOUSE
St Ernan's Island, Donegal
Co Donegal
Tel: 073-21065. $$$
Deluxe hotel on an island, connected by a causeway, charming views of the bay, and a superb menu.

Sligo

THE EMBASSY RESTAURANT
John Kennedy Parade, Sligo
Tel: 071-61250. $$
'New' Irish cuisine on the waterfront overlooking the Garavogue River. Healthy, 'natural' food and efficient service.

REVERIES
Rosses Point, Co Sligo
Tel: 071-77371. $$$
Reservations advised for one of the region's best and most creative restaurants, situated in a charming seaside resort 8km (5 miles) west of Sligo, overlooking Sligo Bay.

BALLINCAR HOUSE HOTEL
Rosses Point Road, Sligo, Co Sligo
Tel: 071-45361. $$
Popular hotel with sports facilities, good seafood restaurant and sound French and Irish cuisine.

MARKREE CASTLE
Collooney, Co Sligo.
Tel: 071 67800. $$$
Imposing pre-Cromwellian castle turned into an imposing hotel. (Salmon fishing available on the river in the estate.)

5. Around Sligo – Yeats Country

We begin this day-long itinerary with a look at Sligo town, followed by a tour around two loughs, Glencar and Lough Gill and the lake isle of Innisfree immortalised by Yeats. On to Parkes Castle, then the sculpture fantasy trail of Hazelwood, followed by a visit to the Carrowmore megalithic graves and the tomb of the legendary Queen Maeve at Knocknarea.

Our day begins in **Sligo** itself, a town ravaged and burned in the 1641 rebellion, though the silver bell from the ancient abbey was saved by being stealthily hauled off and deposited beneath the waters of Lough Gill. They say only the pure of heart can hear its peal from the bottom of the lake. The **Dominican Abbey** ruins, dating from the 13th century, are well preserved and are the only vestige of the medieval town remaining. The **museum** (Stephen Street; June to September, Tuesday to Saturday, 10.30am–12.30pm and 2.30–4.30pm) has an interesting medley of exhibits with objects of local interest plus manuscripts, memorabilia, the Nobel medal and correspondence of W B Yeats.

Our journey begins with a diversion of 8km (5 miles) out to **Rosses Point** where the Yeats brothers used to spend their summers at Elsinore Lodge. Today Rosses Point is a typical seaside village with a small pier for boat trips set between the two superb beaches. Returning to Sligo we take the northeasterly N16. Some 14km (8¾ miles) on, we turn left at a signpost that says 'Waterfall'. This takes us along the shores of **Glencar Lough** in the Partry Mountains, a beautiful drive. At the eastern end are two fine waterfalls, one of which leaps some 20m (65ft). Nearby is the Swiss Valley, a spectacular wooded ravine. By working our way to the right after Glencar Lough, we return to the N16 and continue on until

Carrowmore dolmen

we reach the right-hand turn, the R286, which takes us to **Parkes Castle** (daily, June to September, 10am–6pm), which is set on the shore of Lough Gill. This spectacular lake, 8km (5 miles) long, contains a number of islands, including **Innisfree** where we can reflect on Yeats' words and attain a 'peace that comes dropping slow'.

Over the last eight years Parkes Castle has been authentically restored using old building methods. Its current look of a fortified manor house is owed to a planter, Captain Parke, who was awarded the estate after it was confiscated from the O'Rourke family. From here we continue west on the R286 along the shores of Lough Gill to **Hazelwood**, where a forest trail holds a number of surprises. Dotted along the paths amongst the trees are wooden sculptures ranging from legendary figures and charioteers to some astonishing art nouveau concepts. The **Hazelwood Sculpture Trail** harmonises man's efforts with the quiet beauty of the lakeside wood. To the right, a 10-minute walk up the hillside is the **Deerpark megalithic complex** with a court tomb and souterrain surrounded by a stone cashel (early fort).

For lunch and then more archaeology, we return to Sligo town on the R286. For a filling and inexpensive meal try Beezie's pub in O'Connell Street. After lunch we turn right at John Street. Some 3km (1¼ miles) later we turn left and the acreages of **Carrowmore** begin. The first sight is a particularly fine dolmen in a field on the left. The visitor centre is 1km (half a mile) or so further on. In the 19th century there were some 150 neolithic graves here. Only 60 remain in varying stages of preservation. For the past few years a Swedish team has been excavating the site that includes tombs, stone circles and sepulchral chambers. They have dated the site to around 3300BC. On our journey from Sligo, your curiosity will have been aroused by the large mountain to the west with a very sizeable mound upon its summit. **Knocknarea** is capped by a vast cairn, similar in size and style to Newgrange (Itinerary 2). This is reputed to be the tomb of **Queen Maeve** of Connacht, who lived in the 1st century AD, though it actually contains the remains of earlier occupants dating from around 2000BC. If you have not had any exercise today then this is the moment to pay your respects to Queen Maeve. The walk, following the signposted track, takes about 35 minutes. But the real reason for coming are the panoramas that sweep across Sligo Bay to the Ox Mountains in one direction and Benbulben in the other.

Piling up the peat

Atlantic coast graveyard

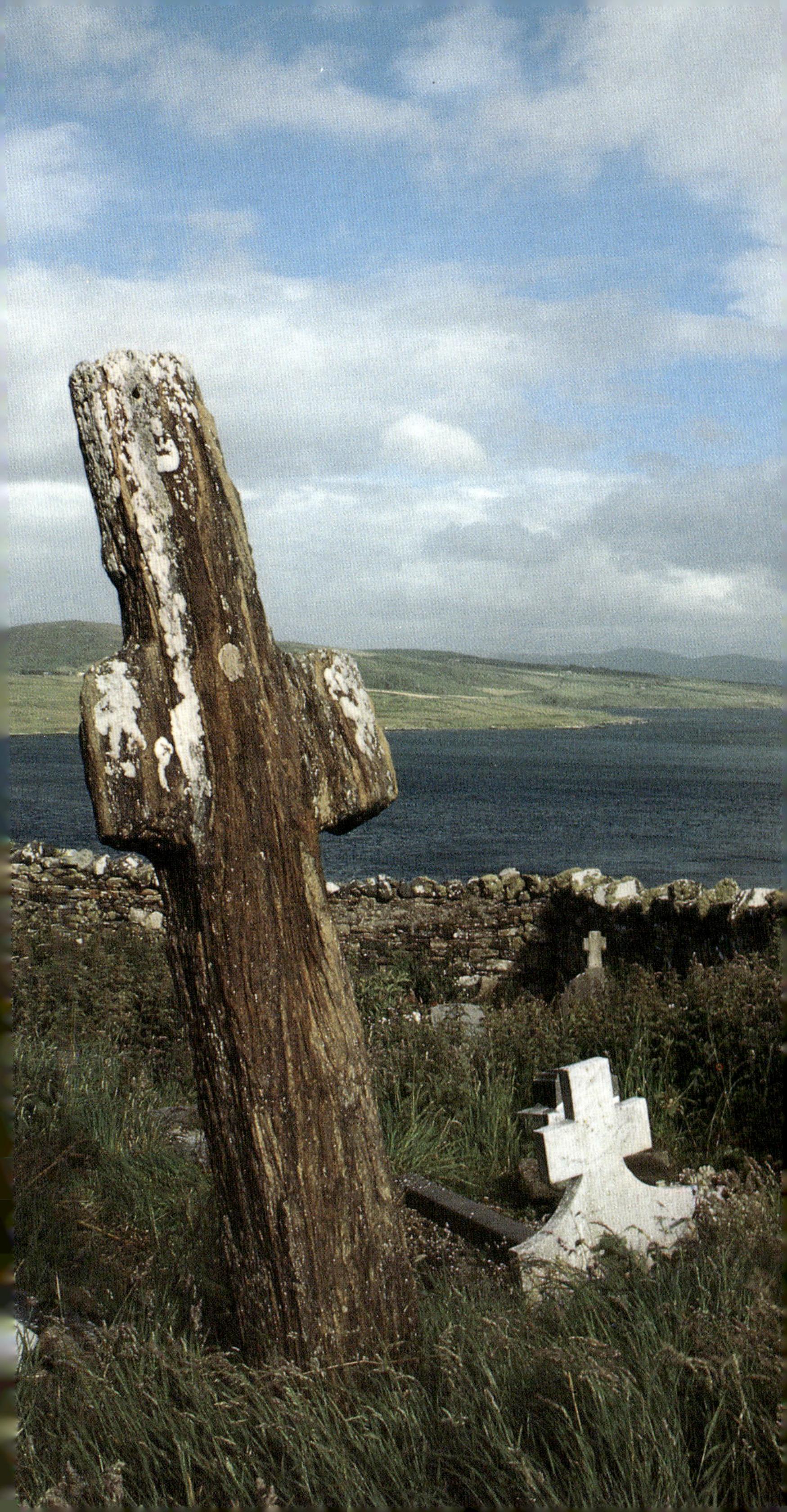

The Far West

6. Westport

Westport is one of Ireland's most enchanting towns. This day divides into two parts: we begin the morning exploring Westport's 18th-century charms before heading north along the shore of Clew Bay to Croagh Patrick, Ireland's holiest mountain. A spectacular drive takes us to the village of Leenane, made famous by the movie *The Field*, before we return for lunch in one of Westport's superb fish restaurants. In the afternoon, we head west for the tropical ambience and wild flowers of Achill Island.

This is not one of those guidebooks that belittles **Westport's** classic looks. The tree-lined mall on either side of the river and the spacious Octagon, the eight-sided market place with its radiating streets and its wide main boulevard, are its centre-pieces. The town was specially designed at the end of the 18th century for the Marquess of Sligo. No-one quite knows who the architect was but the elegant buildings, combining a sense of space and grace, hint towards an unknown Frenchman taken prisoner-of-war from General Humbert's ill-fated army of 1798. The jewel of the town is the 18th-century **Westport House** (July and August, Monday to Saturday, 10.30am–6pm; mid-May to mid-September, Monday to Saturday, 2–5pm, Sunday 2–6pm). The main house has a collection of landscape and portrait paintings but children prefer the grounds, zoo, leisurely boat-trips and picnics by the lake.

After exploring Westport, our journey takes us west on the R395 along Clew Bay, which is peppered with inlets and islands. Some 10km

Westport, County Mayo

(6¼ miles) out of Westport, on the left, is the car park for Ireland's holiest mountain, **Croagh Patrick**. This cone-shaped peak reaches up almost 800m (2,600ft) towards the heavens and is where St Patrick is believed to have fasted during the 40 days of Lent in the year AD441. The cliff face above the car park is where St Patrick is said to have rung his bell to summon all of Ireland's venomous creatures, which he then cast into eternity via the precipice. The last Sunday in July, known as Crom Dubhs Sunday, is when pilgrims gather to climb the summit, often barefoot. Whilst piety envelopes Croagh Patrick at all times, an equally tenacious material crusade is being waged here by a mining consortium, who would rip the mountain asunder for its gold!

The road along Clew Bay, with its views of Clare Island, offers many a turning to small bathing beaches divided by the rocks of the seashore. At **Louisburg** you have the option of turning westward across the moorland road to **Roonah Quay**. This short scenic deviation offers the opportunity of a boat ride to mountainous **Clare Island**, with its harbour overlooked by the castle, once a fortress of the sea queen Grace O'Malley. Legends of her freebooting exploits, fleeting marriage, challenges to England's navy and subsequent allegiance to Queen Elizabeth I are still plentiful. Returning to Louisburg, we turn right on the R395 and pass Lough Doo, a long silvery lake where mountains rise on both sides to over 700m (2,300ft). This journey is beautiful and, in the narrow defile, your breath may be taken away, not just by the landscape but also by the narrow passage which the road takes alongside the river. Descend to **Killary Harbour**, an inlet cut like a fjord into the sur-

Keem Strand, Achill Island

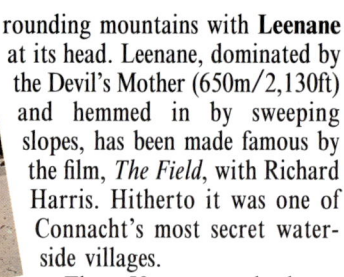

rounding mountains with **Leenane** at its head. Leenane, dominated by the Devil's Mother (650m/2,130ft) and hemmed in by sweeping slopes, has been made famous by the film, *The Field*, with Richard Harris. Hitherto it was one of Connacht's most secret waterside villages.

The N59 turns us back towards Westport, 32km (20 miles) away. Imposing as the journey is, between the Partry Mountains on the right and the Sheffry Hills opposite, the moorland road offers little incentive to punctuate the drive, so we will head straight for Westport anticipating a seafood lunch at one of the restaurants on the quay overlooking Clew Bay. After lunch we leave Westport for **Newport** on the winding N59. This fine village rises above the river and is a fishing centre for the nearby loughs of Feeagh, Furnace and Beltra. On Friday the main street is filled with bustle, conversation and the sound of sheep. Our first stop is at **Burrishoole Abbey** set on a small promontory where two creeks meet. It was founded in the 15th century by the Dominicans and is a charming, lonely ruin in a delightful setting.

We head on to Mulrany (also called Mallaranny) on the narrow isthmus that joins up with the Curraun Peninsula. The meeting of the two bays, coupled with the protection of the mountains, has created an extremely mild climate, particularly noticeable in spring, which brings an early show of wild flowers, and in late summer when the fuchsia bursts into bloom, boxing in homes with walls of shiny crimson pendulums. Giant sub-tropical gunnera plants have also lost their inhibitions here and rampage along ditches to vie with the bog itself. Once over the causeway bridge we arrive on **Achill Island** where we follow the Atlantic Drive signs taking us clockwise round the island. **Kildownet Castle** is a fine tower standing on the rocky beach. Further on is a small sad cemetery, a result of the 'great hunger' and a shipping tragedy in Clew Bay. A little way on, the road takes to the cliffs and begins to switchback, offering superb coastal views. To the south there are good views of Clare Island.

At Dooega (Dumha Eige) the road turns inland for 5km (3 miles) or so before turning left for Keel and Dooagh. **Keel** shows signs that, lonely as we imagined the road to be, other holidaymakers have come this way as well. The beach, with its giant caravan site, destroys the illusion of solitude. Further on is **Dooagh** with the famous Keem Strand beach backed by the peak of Croaghaun. This is also where Captain Boycott had a lodge. His name is now in the dictionary, because he was totally ostracised by local people when working as a landlord's agent in the 1770s, whilst Charles Stewart Parnell adopted his name as a tactic in the struggle against

The Peak of Croaghaun

landlordism. Here the road ends and we can continue on a healthy walk to **Achill Head**, looking to the right to the 650m (2,100ft) cliff that rises out of the sea almost to the top of Croaghaun. Our journey back follows the Atlantic Drive route signs. To sample the rural tranquillity of the area, simply turn off and follow a side road, such as the one for **Dugort**. The way back also means sharing the road with sheep and cattle munching on the verges. There are also areas where turf cutters can be seen cutting the peat. The journey offers views across Achill Sound and deep into County Mayo. The final descent into Achill is thick with rhododendrons before we meet the causeway bridge, which takes us back via Mulrany to Westport.

Hotels and Restaurants

ASGARD TAVERN and RESTAURANT
The Quay, Westport, Co Mayo
Tel: 098-25319. **$/$$**
Inexpensive bar food in the tavern and seafood in the restaurant above.

QUAY COTTAGE
The Quay, Westport, Co Mayo
Tel: 098-26412. **$$**
Lively and informal wine bar decorated with fishing tackle and an excellent seafood restaurant.

OLD RAILWAY HOTEL
The Mall, Westport, Co Mayo
Tel: 098-25166. **$$**
Authentic Victorian décor, inexpensive lunches and bar meals, homely restaurant and a lively, popular bar, often with live music.

ARDMORE HOUSE RESTAURANT
The Quay, Westport, Co. Mayo
Tel: 098-25994. **$/$$**
Family-run restaurant serving locally caught seafood and game. (Bar menu available too.)

Leenane

7. Connemara

This circular drive from Galway can be done in a day or, if you adopt the more leisurely pace of rural Ireland, you could take two. It takes us through some of the strangest and most beautiful scenery in the far west of Ireland, a region with an unsurpassed sense of remoteness. Highlights include the Connemara National Park, the Alcock and Brown memorial and numerous timeless fishing villages.

'There is nowhere like Connemara'; so the saying goes. To some the landscape is melancholic; to others it is distinctive, those for whom lonesome scenery is the epitome of peace. **Connemara** offers itself openly to all interpretations. To one person's eye, the hallmarks are its shapes and colours; the varying pewters of ever-present water and stone; walls and rocky outcrops swelling out in lumps and bumps from an intense green turf, occasionally splashed white by a solitary cottage. To others it may be the variety of russets on the slopes of the rugged peaks of the Maamturk Mountains cut by so many valleys, lakes and rivers; or the flat, saw-toothed coastline of rocky promontories joined by sandy, shell-filled coves.

Our first drive in Connemara takes us away from the buzz and bustle of Galway to Oughterard along the shores of mighty **Lough Corrib**. It seems fitting to muse upon the words, 'Westward ho, let us rise with the sun and be off to the land of the west', as we drive along the N59 before turning right to visit **Aughnanure Castle** (daily, mid-June to mid-September, 9.30am–6.30pm), 25km (15½ miles) from the city centre. This is a splendid castle, well signposted, which has been expertly restored and rests nobly beside a stream.

From Aughnanure Castle we return to the main road, turning right in Oughterard, then almost immediately left over the bridge, to begin a journey along the lakeshore with its inlets, islets and boathouses, set amongst wild fuchsia hedges. The road ends after 12km (7½ miles) at a little-used car park beside the water. From here you can enjoy the view of the Hill O'Doon as depicted on postcards.

Turning round we retrace our journey for some 8km (5 miles), looking for a lane, signposted 'Scenic Route', on our right. This not only cuts out the return to Oughterard but takes us cross-country and offers superb views back onto the lake. At the N59 we turn right for **Maam Cross**.

Aughnanure Castle

Maam Cross on market day

This remote hamlet set in the shadow of Leckavrea Mountain is the district centre for roadside markets and gatherings. Stop if something is going on as this is a wonderful chance to encounter local people, before continuing along the valley to **Sraith Salach** (also known as **Recess**). This hamlet surrounded by lakes has an excellent craft shop offering items made from the local marble.

Next we turn right on the R344. The road gently climbs into the hills, over a saddle and down along the shores of Lough Inagh, a particularly beautiful drive. At the junction with the N59 we turn left towards Letterfrack, following another valley with the Twelve Pins Mountains on our left. The last of the three lakes that stretch 8km (5 miles) on the Dawros River reveals **Kylemore Abbey** (daily, 10am–6pm). This appears to grow from amongst the lakeshore trees in the mountain's shadow. Its many towers and battlements, built in the 1860s, reflect the grandeur and fantasy of brash Balmoral-Gothic architecture. Today it is a convent school run by Benedictine Nuns, but visitors can enjoy the chapel and grounds, as well as the restaurant and the shop selling the nuns' pottery.

Clifden Town

Some 5km (3 miles) beyond lies **Letterfrack**, a charming village at the head of Barnaderg Bay, founded by the Quakers in the 19th century, whilst on our left is Connemara National Park, with its expanse of fine boglands, mountains and heaths. The visitor centre (daily, April to October, 10am–6pm) gives comprehensive details of the park's features from flora and fauna to geology, hiking trails and climbs.

Our route now takes us out to the 'moonscapes' of Connemara, where rocky outcrops break out from the vivid greens of the turf and whitewashed cottages tuck themselves away amongst the boulders. From here we are filled with a sense of remoteness and of wonder that anyone could till such tough terrain. The Irish saying 'To Hell or to Connacht' becomes logical. Some 3km (1¼ miles) out of Letterfrack, we turn right following the sign to **Cleggan**, a small fishing village where you can take a boat ride out to Inishbofin Island. We continue to follow the road around the peninsula with its tiny sandy bays between the rocky, seaweed-clad fingers that stretch far into the sea. This is where the seashore beckons; rockpools are filled with shrimps, the wet sands are loaded with razor clams, whilst a probe beneath a seaweed-encrusted stone shelf might just reveal the dark iridescent hue of a tasty lobster.

Irish fishing boats, 'curraghs'

Our peninsula circuit brings us next to **Clifden**, dominated by its two church spires, perched in its high mountain valley setting above an inlet of Ardbear Bay. This is the main town of Connemara, attracting artists, mountaineers, sea anglers, salmon fishermen, the famous Connemara pony breeders and stone masons for the marble.

There is little of historic interest in this alpine-like town, which was only founded in the 19th century, but it is worth staying here just for the excellent restaurants serving local lobsters, oysters, langoustines and mussels. Whether or not you spend the night here, our journey now takes us south from Clifden on the R341.

Just beyond Ballyconneely is the **Alcock and Brown Transatlantic Landing Site**. This is a memorial commemorating the first transatlantic flight, made in the wood and fabric-covered Vickers Vimy. On 15 June 1919, the two aviators landed here, tipping their biplane onto its nose in the bog after 16 hours and 12 minutes of daring flight.

Alcock and Brown memorial

Next we just continue flowing along the coast to **Roundstone** with its harbour towered over by Mount Errisbeg. Like all Connemara's fishing villages, there is little to see here in the way of ruins, little evidence of momentous history. These tiny places have had hardships enough without those of blood and battle. Even so, these villages are a picturesque joy to see and time can be spent dwelling upon their peaceful lifestyles. Beyond Roundstone lies Toombe-

Galway city

ola with its ruined abbey. Here we turn right onto the R342 to **Cashel**. The strange Connemara coastline still flanks the road. Peeling off onto any side track to the right, we will arrive at shell-encrusted beaches all our own, not another soul in sight.

From the lobster port of Carna, the road sweeps us around to **Kilkieran (Cill Ciaráin)** where St Kiernan is said to have come ashore. His holy well is in the cemetery and every September the village becomes a centre for pilgrims. Beyond lie Derryrush and Gortmore (An Gort Mór) with its peat-burning power station and, within 3km (1¾ miles), we turn right onto the R336 towards Costelloe (Casla) with its radio station that broadcasts only in Gaelic. Our journey continues along the north shore of Galway Bay, passing through the coastal villages of Inverin (Indreabhán), Spiddal (An Spidéal) and Barna (Bearna), before we experience the culture shock of being in a city once again.

Today **Galway** is a vigorous regional industrial and commercial centre. Its history is not yet lost and the focal point is the wide and open Eyre Square with its cascading fountain and the John F Kennedy Memorial Garden. The tourist office in the square has details of a number of walking tours that would include the **Church of St Nicholas** (1320). It is said that Christopher Columbus prayed here before his epic voyage. Lynch's Castle sadly underwent a horrific modernisation in the 1960s. Probably the most surprising sight in the city, whose yesterdays are fast being obscured, are the salmon waiting below **Salmon Weir Bridge** near the cathedral, before leaping the weir to make their way up to Lough Corrib. The **Old Jail site**, with its black marble archway, features a skull and crossbones in memory of the merciless Judge Lynch, who condemned and hanged his own son in the late 15th century. On a more romantic note is the **Claddagh Ring**, with its heart and two clasped hands, part of the original city walls, also known as the Spanish Gate.

Hotels
Clifden

ROCK GLEN MANOR HOUSE
Clifden, Co Galway
Tel: 095-21035. $$/$$$
Country-life atmosphere in a converted hunting lodge. The hotel also has a good restaurant serving fresh local produce.

ABBEYGLEN CASTLE HOTEL
Sky Road, Clifden, Co Galway
Tel: 095-21201. $$/$$$
Gourmet cuisine, especially oysters and lobster. Piano playing; wide views of Clifden and the sea.

Galway

ARDILAUN HOUSE
Taylor's Hill, Galway, Co Galway
Tel: 091-21433. $$
Ardilaun House is perfect for those who like peace and quiet, with a pleasant garden and restaurant.

GREAT SOUTHERN
Eyre Square, Galway, Co Galway
Tel: 091-64041. $$$
Imposing 19th-century railway hotel with Victorian ambience but mod cons as well, such as the heated rooftop swimming pool. The Oyster Room restaurant is Galway's most elegant dining room.

SKEFFINGTON ARMS
28 Eyre Square, Galway, Co Galway
Tel: 091-63173. $$
Hotel with a sense of history.

Restaurants
Clifden

D'ARCY INN
Main Street, Clifden, Co Galway
Tel: 095-21146. $$
Seafood and lobsters in profusion at a reasonable price.

DORIS'S
Clifden, Co Galway
Tel: 095-21427. $$
Multi-national cuisine to the accompaniment of harp music.

O'GRADY'S
Clifden, Co Galway
Tel: 095-21450. $$
Well-established family business operating its own fishing boat for the freshest Atlantic produce. It serves lobster and steamed clams.

Galway

CONLAN'S
Eglington Street, Galway, Co Galway
Tel: 091-62268. $
Inexpensive (no credit cards), serving the freshest fish and oysters in a simple café-style basement below the takeaway area.

DRIMCONG HOUSE
Moycullen (Maigh Cuilinn)
Co Galway. Tel: 091-85115. $$$
Located in the village of Moycullen, 19km (11¾ miles) northwest along the N59 Oughterard road and worth the drive (book in advance). Owner/chef Gerry Galvin is regarded as one of Ireland's best, noted for oysters, black pudding and vegetables.

NOCTAN'S
17 Cross Street, Galway, Co Galway
Tel: 091-66172. $
Artists' hangout with a limited but excellent menu of whatever is best in the market that day, including vegetarian dishes.

GBC RESTAURANT
7 Williamsgate Street
Galway, Co Galway
Tel: 091-63087. $$
Welcoming restaurant in a period house. Seafood, poultry and vegetarian cuisine.

The Mid West

8. The Burren

This day-long itinerary takes us from Galway to Limerick across the glaciated uplands of The Burren, where there are over 400 historic forts, and arctic and tropical plants growing side by side. We visit the Burren Display Centre, Kilfenora Cathedral and the high crosses, the spa town of Lisdoonvarna with its Festival of Match-Making, the Cliffs of Moher and Ennis Abbey before reaching Limerick, the major city in the mid-west of Ireland.

Travelling in style

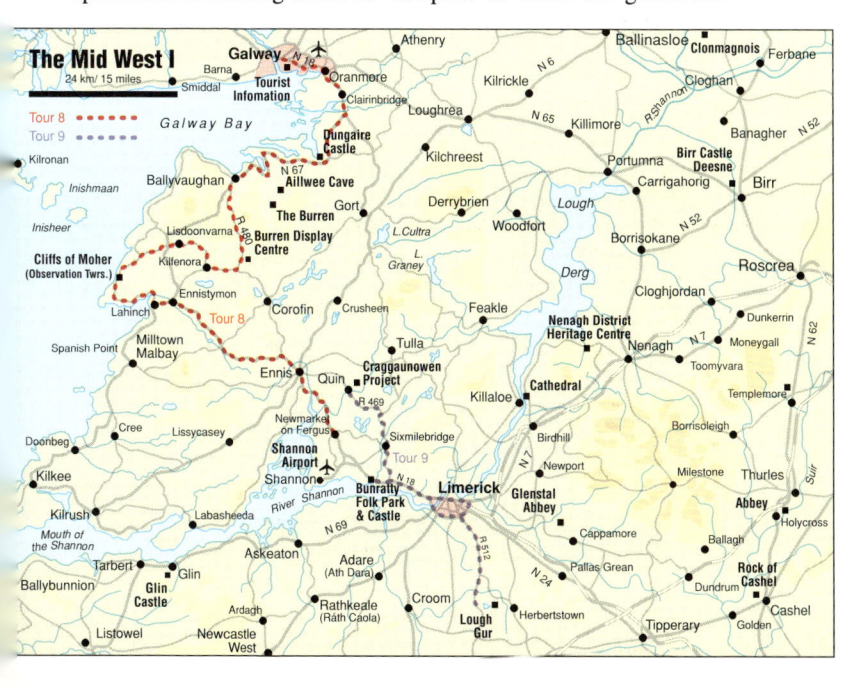

Leaving Galway southwards by the combined N18/N67, we pass the late Paddy Burke's tavern in **Clarinbridge** where he founded the world-famous Galway Oyster Festival that occurs each September. At Kilcolgan we branch right on the N67 for the curiosity of **Dungaire Castle**. The 16th-century tower, in its idyllic waterside setting, specialises in hosting medieval banquets at which the guests are entertained by 'light-hearted' extracts from Synge, Yeats and Gogarty. The phrase 'light-hearted', in relation to these authors, seems rather a contradiction. Call 061-61788 to book places at a local banquet. The harbour is a delight and worthy of a pause for its traditional sailboats – Galway Bay hookers are often moored along the quay. Some 20km (12½ miles) on, we pass through **Ballyvaughan** and head south, on the R480 Corofin road, to reach the **Aillwee Caves** (daily, April to September 10am–6pm). It is said that the caves were discovered as far back as 1896, although the story here is that a farmer found them by accident in 1944 while looking for his lost dog. Even more impressive than the guided tour – through passages, into stalactitic chambers and past waterfalls – is the visitor centre itself. Moulded into the terrain, the stone-faced structure has won many awards, not just for its exterior but for the interior layout with its coffee and gift shop. Before leaving the car park it is worth looking over the parapet down onto a string of earthen ring forts.

Shortly beyond Aillwee, as we continue on the R480, we start to experience the strangeness of **The Burren** with its swirling limestone terraces. The Burren is an area, 500km^2 (193 square miles) in size, of sedimentary limestone and shell from an ancient seabed that has risen 300m (1,000ft) and then suffered the tortures of glacial action. Smoothed by ice and the elements, the gnarled and fissured pavements have become home to a unique flora and fauna. Underground rivers abound, rushing below the surface with over 60km (37¼ miles) of known pot-holing tunnels and caverns. The unusual geological formation has produced not only an astonishing variety of vegetation, some unique to The Burren, but was also a busy habitat for neolithic man. Cairns, court graves and dolmens abound, including some 400 stone forts (*cashels*). The only wonder is how they tilled such rock!

Over 125 different types of plant thrive here including 22 species of orchid. The Burren also has some unique butterfly species. Botanists from all over the world scurry around The Burren in springtime, amazed that plants from the four zones – Arctic, Alpine, Temperate and Tropical – flourish here side by side. May and June are the real months of glory, when the gentians, mountain avens and bloody cranesbills bloom.

The views to the right across Galway Bay are another sensation. If scouring The Burren's slopes with binoculars, look out for herds of wild goat and the elusive pine marten. Another noticeable feature are the 'holed walls' which allow the wind through, differing in style every few hundred metres depending on the maker's way. Built in the famine of the 1840s, some enclosures are miniscule; hereditary laws stated that land had to be bequeathed to every child in equal measure, so plots had to be divided into smaller and smaller allotments. The road takes us past the famous **Poulnabrone Dolmen**, a portal tomb which dates to 4000BC. Although the dolmen has been made famous by numerous photographs, there is no sign but it is easily spotted from the road.

As the road descends from the high Burren plateau we see **Leamaneh Castle**, a stronghold of the O'Briens. The castle was built in two phases: the tower in 1480 and the fortified manor, with its mullioned windows, in 1640. In 1651 after Conor O'Brien was killed in battle his body was brought back to the castle. Maura Rua MacMahon, his colourful and notorious wife, refused the servants permission to take her dead husband inside, saying, 'We want no dead men here!' Infrequently visited by tourists, it is well worth a look, especially the fine stone stairway in the tower. We turn right, at this crossroad, and take the R476 for **Kilfenora**, once an ecclesiastical capital. The **Burren Display Centre** (daily, June to August, 9.30am–7.30pm; March to May and September to October, 10am–5.30pm) is a 'must-do'; a scale model of the region explains the geology, scenery, flora and fauna very effectively through the medium of a sound and light show. It also covers many of the region's historical sites, which we would not otherwise see without tramping over the hills for weeks. The presentation is first-rate, as are the tea rooms on-site.

Adjacent to the centre, in this tiny village, is the 12th-century **cathedral**, founded on the monastery site of St Fachtna. The walls display carvings, effigies of bishops from the 13th and 14th centuries and other curious embellishments. There are four high crosses; the most interesting is the Doorty Cross showing three bishops with different croziers.

Our journey now takes us on to **Lisdoonvarna**, a spa town popular in the Victorian era for its iron, magnesium and sulphur baths. The **Spa-Wells Health Centre** serves heated sulphur water for drinking, whilst the Bath House offers sauna and pampering treatments, followed by an old-time lunch-time dance session (both open daily, June to October,

10am–6pm). In September the town goes in for a month-long party with its **Match-Making festival**. This is a legacy from the days when hard-working rural farmers came to town after the harvest for a little 'yo-ho' and, hopefully, to find a wife. For lunch, try the Orchid Room restaurant in Steedy's Spa View Hotel (Tel: 065-74026) where the inexpensive, French-inspired cooking is outstanding.

From here we take the coast road to the **Cliffs of Moher**, one of County Clare's most renowned features. The cliffs rise 200m (650ft) vertically from the Atlantic breakers and stretch for some 7km (4¼ miles). Standing back from the edge you have an excellent view of the Aran Islands and viewing them sideways you can see the varying colours of the differing rock strata. Looking down upon fulmars, kittiwakes, puffins, razorbills and rare choughs is a dizzying experience. The crowded Moher Visitor Centre offers tourist information, a cafe and a bureau de change.

The final part of our drive takes us on the R478 to **Ennistymon**, with its colourful shop fronts, scenic waterful and the lively Archway Tavern, and on to the N85 to **Ennis** with its striking Franciscan Abbey founded in 1250. The friary's main features are the De Valera Museum and Library with its collection of antiquities. From here we head straight along the N18 to Limerick or rather, if you are in an indulgent five-star mood, to the luxurious Dromoland Castle Hotel (Newmarket-on-Fergus, 10km/6¼ miles south of Ennis off the N18).

The Cliffs of Moher

Hotels and Restaurants
Adare

Adare is a charming but pricey village 16km (10 miles) southwest of Limerick on the N21 and makes an ideal base for those who prefer peace and quiet to the bustle and shabbiness of Limerick.

ADARE MANOR
Adare, Co Limerick
Tel: 061-396566. $$$
Country house hotel set in a vast Victorian Gothic pile. Huge, antique-studded rooms, swimming pool, riding, fishing, golf; and live music nightly in summer.

MUSTARD SEED
Main Street, Adare, Co Limerick
Tel: 061-396451. $$$
Modern gourmet Irish cuisine in a quaint, cluttered cottage.

Clarinbridge

PADDY BURKE'S
Clarinbridge, Co Galway
Tel: 091-96107. $$$
Eight kilometres (5 miles) south of Galway on the N18, this former tavern is now a world-famous oyster bar and seafood restaurant. The late Paddy Burke put Galway on the map when he founded the annual oyster festival (September). Reservations are essential here in high summer.

Limerick

JURY'S
Ennis Road, Limerick, Co Limerick
Tel: 061-327777. $$$
Modern, but central and quiet hotel with sports and fishing facilities.

RESTAURANT DE LA FONTAINE
12 Gerald Griffin Street, Limerick Co Limerick. Tel: 061-414461. $$
Authentic *cuisine de grandemère* in a converted warehouse in the city centre. Reservations advised.

Newmarket-on-Fergus

DROMOLAND CASTLE
Newmarket-on-Fergus, Co Clare
Tel: 061-368144. $$$
Deluxe hotel set in the ancestral home of Conor O'Brien, direct descendant of Brian Boru who defeated the Vikings in 1014. The hotel has enormous antique-filled rooms, splendid views over the 1,000-acre estate, a golf course and a majestic dining room.

9. Limerick Interlude

Thanks to Shannon International Airport, Limerick and environs have no shortage of tourist attractions. After the lonely beauty of Ireland's far west, the sights of Limerick may strike you as somewhat contrived. Even so, each sight has its merits, so relax and spend a day enjoying such themed introductions to Ireland's heritage as the Craggaunowen Project at Quin, the Bunratty Folk Park and Castle, the well-restored King John's Castle in Limerick and the Lough Gur Stone Age Project.

The **Craggaunowen Project** (daily, April to October, 10am–6pm) at **Quin** (20km/12½ miles north of Limerick on the R469) is a re-creation of life in neolithic times, inspired by the late historian and archaeologist, John Hunt.

The most striking feature is the **Crannog**, or lake-dwelling complex, with its wattle and daub houses. There is also a ring fort with souterrain. It is thought that there were once some 40,000 similar settlements throughout Ireland.

Another tableau is a cooking site of the type often used on hunting trips as well as in settlements. Pits were dug into the marshy ground where water would seep; baked stones were then thrown in to heat the water. Water was kept at very high temperatures by the addition of more hot stones. One genuine artefact is the 2,000-year-old wooden track-way removed for preservation from Longford. Also on display is a replica of the **Brendan Boat**, built by Tim Severin, who sailed across the Atlantic in support of his theory that St Brendan reached the shores of the New World in the 6th century. The centre-piece of Craggaunowen is the castle itself, dating from 1550. It was one of more than 80 constructed in County Clare. The castle interior has been authentically furnished.

Brendan Boat

Bunratty (10km/6¼ miles west of Limerick on the N18; daily, 9.30am–5.30pm) is, despite all the 'hoopla', another thought-provoking experience and not to be avoided because of the charter bus groups. The castle (daily, 9.30am–4.30pm), dating back to 1277, has seen turbulent times and much fighting before its walls. It has been rebuilt a number of times but the present structure dates to 1450. Like Craggaunowen it has been restored and furnished with items befitting the period. Consider booking a place at the evening medieval banquet, the best in Ireland, hosted by celebrated singers and entertainers.

19th-century shops in the Folk Park

The **Folk Park** in the castle grounds (daily, 9.30am–7pm), depicts Irish lifestyles through the ages. Cottages have been furnished accurately whether from Connemara or Kerry. There is an authentic 19th-century village with working craft shops and general stores in which the serving staff wear period costume. The significance of the changes that have taken place in Irish rural life came home to me here when I overheard a young mother, in her mid-thirties, talking to her son of eight dressed in baseball cap and jeans. 'It is not so long ago – in fact it was just 20 years – when mother threw out the old kettle above the peat fire and we got a range,' she recalled. 'Two years later the electricity came and we got a stove, but still the washing water came from the barrel.' The boy smiled.

Outside Bunratty is **Durty Nelly's pub**, touristy but well worth visiting to slake the thirst. In Limerick itself it is essential to see **King John's Castle** (open daily, 9.30am–5.30pm), a medieval fortress with an imaginative new exhibition tracing the history of Limerick. Some 17km (10½ miles) south of the city, well signed from the R512, is **Lough Gur**, one of the most important archaeological sites in Ireland, with definitive evidence of man's existence here from 3000BC through to medieval times.

10. Limerick to Tralee

A day-long journey southwards from Limerick visiting Adare, which is considered to be Ireland's loveliest village, Matrix Castle, where possibly the first potatoes in Ireland were cultivated, Ardagh, famous for its Chalice, Foynes with its Flying Boat Museum and Castleisland with the Crag Cave system.

Before leaving Limerick, call in at the **Hunt Collection** at Limerick University (weekdays, 9am–5pm) (This fine collection of early Celtic treasures can be seen at the Old Custom House from autumn 1995. Afterwards spend some time walking the wide streets of the fourth largest city in Ireland, founded by the Danes in the 9th century. Historically it has had its sieges and

Thatched cottage, Adare

battles from the time Brian Boru took it from the Danes. After the Battle of the Boyne in 1690, the Irish holed up in King John's Castle **Limerick Castle** for over a year until surrendering with honour, after which the famous Treaty of Limerick was signed, beginning the exodus and banishment of Irish chiefs, nobles and soldiers, who became known as the 'Wild Geese'. There are excellent walking tours of the city, some of them guided; ask for details from the tourist office in Arthur's Quay (Tel: 061-333644). Leaving Limerick we travel southwest on the N21 to **Adare (Ath Dara)**, an old-world village with an English look. Limes and oaks fringe the main street and the thatched cottages are made picturesque by their creepers and abundant herbaceous borders, halting in a crush of colour at garden walls. Adare has no less than three abbeys. The Trinitarian Abbey, founded in 1230, is partly restored and in use, the Augustinian Priory dates to 1315 and the Franciscan Friary, of 1464, now stands in the heart of the Golf Club, along with Desmond Castle. Before driving on, consider a cup of coffee or lunch in the 1830s Gothic Revival Adare Manor.

Smooth countryside lies alongside the N21 to **Rathkeale** where there are the remains of an Augustinian priory. Certainly worth stopping for is **Castle Matrix** (May to September, Saturday to Tuesday, 1–5pm), 3km (1¾ miles) along on the right, privately owned by Sean O'Driscoll, an American architect, who has restored the castle and furnished it authentically. It is the oldest inhabited castle in Ireland. Back on the N21 we turn right for **Ardagh** where, in 1868, the famous Celtic chalice and brooch (now in Dublin's National Museum) were discovered in the nearby ring fort, accessible by crossing a field. In contrast is **Foynes**, our next stop. Here the new GPA **Aviation Museum** (July to October, Monday to Saturday, 10am–6pm; Sunday, 2–7pm), which takes its theme from the age of the trans-

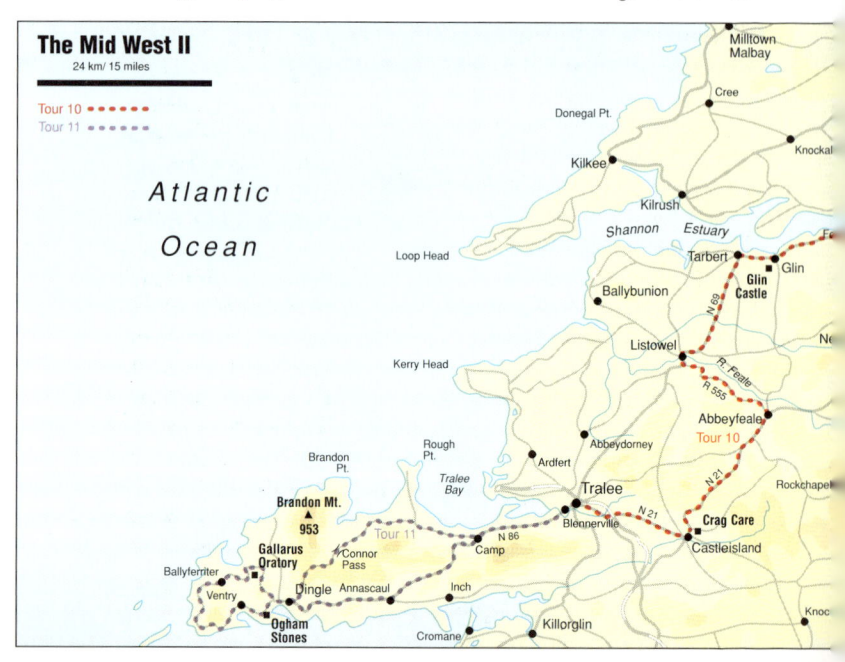

Glin Castle

atlantic flying boats and the great Pan American clippers of the 1930s, has been established.

Our journey continues alongside the Shannon Estuary to **Glin** with its magical castle (May only, 10am–noon and 2–4pm; otherwise by appointment only; Tel: 068-34112) built in 1780, though the embellishments, such as the battlements and mullioned windows, were added in the Victorian era. It is still owned by the Fitz-Gerald family – otherwise known as the Knights of Glin.

Further along the shore is **Tarbert**, where ferries ply to County Clare. Tarbert House is true original Georgian-Irish. There is an excellent collection of period furniture, including Irish Chippendale, and portraits by Irish artists. Next we turn inland, on the N69, to **Listowel**, a market town with the remains of a twin-towered Fitzmaurice castle in the square. The town is proud of having produced many nationally acclaimed writers and stages a well-known literary festival in June.

We continue by taking the R555 to **Abbeyfeale**, then turn right on the N21 to **Castleisland**, a bustling town once the stronghold of the Desmonds. Turn right by the Library and the road leads to the **Crag Cave**, where some 4km (2½ miles) of limestone caves have been surveyed. There is a visitor centre and the guided tour weaves amongst the spikes of stalactites and stalagmites, passing side passages with names from Tolkien's *Lord of the Rings*, such as the 'Hall of Gondor', where sounds of underground streams and rivers echo. Return to Castleisland and take the all-too-easy-to-miss sign, right, at the end of the Main Street, which takes us on the N21 to Tralee.

Hotels and Restaurants

BALLYGARRY HOUSE
Leebrook, Tralee, Co Kerry
Tel: 066-21233. $
Comfortable hotel with a restaurant serving fresh local food.

BRANDON
Princes Street, Tralee, Co Kerry
Tel: 066-23333. $$
Modern town-centre hotel with swimming pool and restaurant.

CHEZ JEAN MARC
29 Castle Street, Tralee, Co Kerry
Tel: 066-21377. $$
Reservations advised for this sophisticated French-style restaurant, noted for its finesse.

BALLYSEEDE CASTLE
Tralee, Co Kerry
Tel: 066-25799. $$
Small hotel (13 rooms) of great character with magnificent rooms.

11. The Dingle Peninsula

This is one of Ireland's most spectacular tours. The road from Tralee takes us out onto the stunning Irish-speaking Dingle Peninsula, where some 2,000 sites of antiquity have been identified. Notable are the beehive stone huts built by the early monks and the Gallarus Oratory. The return journey crosses the Connor Pass where, astride the ridge, there are dramatic vistas on both sides, with Mount Brandon at your elbow. If based in Killarney, Cork or Tralee, you may opt for an organised tour which covers the same route, with the exception of the Connor Pass. If doing this route by car, expect misleading signposting, with wrong distances marked and many names only written in Irish.

After exploring Denny Street and the centre of **Tralee**, with its 18th-century architecture, we head west on the N86. The first point of interest is the windmill with a visitor centre at **Blennerville** (daily, April to October, 10am–5pm), beside the old ship canal. Beyond, the journey's beginning seems totally unpromising as we run along the bland marshy edges of Tralee Bay for some 15km (9¼ miles). However, at **Camp**, the left turn sees us start to climb, offering a bold view sweeping around Castlegregory, Rough Point and out into Tralee Bay. As we ascend the side of the strange mountain of Caherconree, on the left we see that the summit holds an ancient fort that was the reputed home of a legendary hero-god, Curio Mac Daire.

Turn off the road left for **Inch**, the amazing beach – featured in the film *Ryan's Daughter* – with its sandhill dwellings from ancient times. Today it is better known as the location of the liaison between Eamonn Casey, then Bishop of Galway, and an American woman. The discovery of the love-nest and love-child in 1992 had long-lasting social reverberations. Then proceed on to **Annascaul** where the South Pole Inn recalls that a former proprietor was a member of the ill-fated Scott expedition to the Antarctic. We carry on towards Dingle (An Daingean) where, just before at **Ballintaggart**, we turn left and sharp left again at a 'Road Danger' sign to see a small round Celtic cemetery with nine Ogham stones.

The view from Camp

Back to the route and into **Dingle** proper which enjoys new-found wealth as a result of all the visitors who come to see Fungie, the dolphin that came to the harbour in 1985 and has stayed ever since. Local boatmen offer dolphin-spotting trips from Dingle pier. Stories abound locally of the dirty deeds that have been committed by other villages across the bay who have endeavoured to lure the mammal to their waters. Dingle, although surrounded by historic antiquities and early ecclesiastical sites, offers little for the visitor, which is perhaps why Marie Antoinette refused to be rescued from her French jail and brought to Dingle, where she was to be secretly housed in the property on the corner of John and Main streets.

Even so, you may want to stop here for shopping or lunch, if only to sample the resolutely arty-crafty atmosphere. Try **Doyle's Seafood Bar** (John Street; Tel: 066-51174) for excellent and inexpensive dishes.

From Dingle we head out to **Slea Head** on the R539, past Ventry Harbour with its complicated legends of kings, eloping wives, giants, champions, secret trysts, treachery and poets that put the legends of King Arthur to shame by comparison. At **Dunbeg**, some 6km (3¾ miles) from Ventry, is one of the region's many Iron Age coastal forts with a souterrain and stone enclosures, earthen ramparts and ditches. At **Fahan**, some 100m (300ft) above on the right-hand side of the road, for the next 5km (3 miles) there are over 400 *clochans* or beehive cells. These are accessible via farmers' gates but, to see any of the sites near the road, local landowners extract a small fee. Next we simply follow the narrow and awe-inspiring

Inch region, Dingle peninsula

Beehive hut, Fahan

coast road around Slea Head, gazing at coves, beaches and the **Blasket Islands (An Blascaod Mór)**. After **Ballyferriter (Baile an Fheirtéaraigh)** we turn inland. Some 3km (1¼ miles) beyond the village is **Reask**, which can be found by turning right after the bridge. This is an excellent monastic settlement which is worth spending a few minutes to investigate; among other things, look out for its exquisitely cut Pillar Stone.

From here we go back to the road and turn right following the **Gallarus Oratory** signs. Dating from the 8th century, this endearing, boat-shaped structure, built out of rough unhewn stone, was once a chapel. From here, there is a clear view of **Gallarus Castle**, a 15th century tower house near the shore.

At the crossroads above Gallarus we turn left for **Kilmalkedar Church**. Few ever visit this intriguing antiquity. The ruined Romanesque church was built around 1150, although the settlement dates from the 7th century. A number of curious standing stones exist, including an 'Abecedarium' (a Latin alphabet stone), a holed stone, a sundial stone and a crude ancient cross. The Romanesque features and arches have been superbly carved and have hardly weathered over the centuries.

Turning back past Gallarus, we return to Dingle and turn left in the town for the precarious **Connor Pass**, the highest in Ireland. Even if the day is raining or misty you should still make this drive as the weather can be very different once you get to the other side of the peninsula.

At the summit you will be rewarded by one of Europe's most spectacular views; or, as one awed American visitor put it, a panorama 'in the world league…'

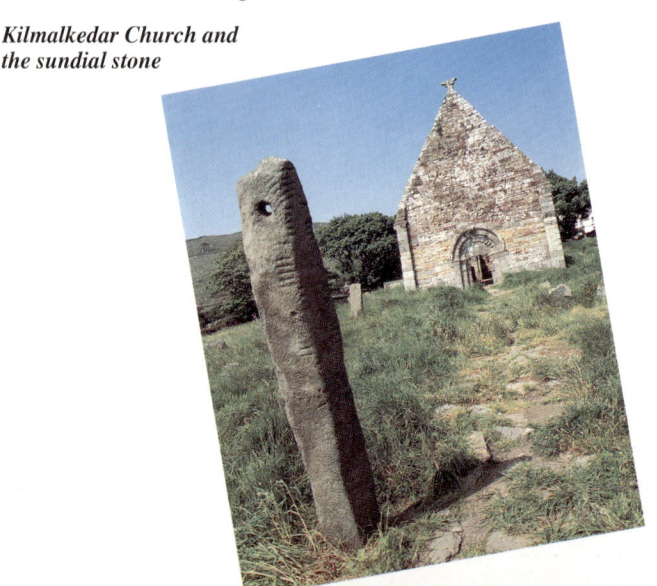

Kilmalkedar Church and the sundial stone

The Southwest

12. Killarney to Bantry

A full day that begins in Killarney, takes us to Muckross House for a horse-drawn car ride, then to Glengarriff and the island paradise of Ilnacullin gardens and finally to Bantry. If tired of driving, take a Lakes of Killarney minibus from Dero's (Tel: 064-31251), opposite Killarney tourist office.

'Top of the morning to you!' If this phrase was ever used in Ireland then Killarney would be the most likely place to expect such a greeting. In order to get some perspective on this most friendly region, I advise driving to the north end of the town by following the signs to **Aghadoe** for some 3km (1¾ miles). From here the panoramic views stretch some 20km (12½ miles) across island-studded **Lough Leane** and on to the **Macgillycuddy's Reeks**.

Worth visiting whilst back in Killarney are the neo-gothic cathedral, and the bustling narrow shopping streets, which are open until 10pm in summer. The town has several good restaurants and pubs which stand out from the tourist traps. Consider lunch or dinner at Bricin, a homely traditional restaurant in the High Street – or

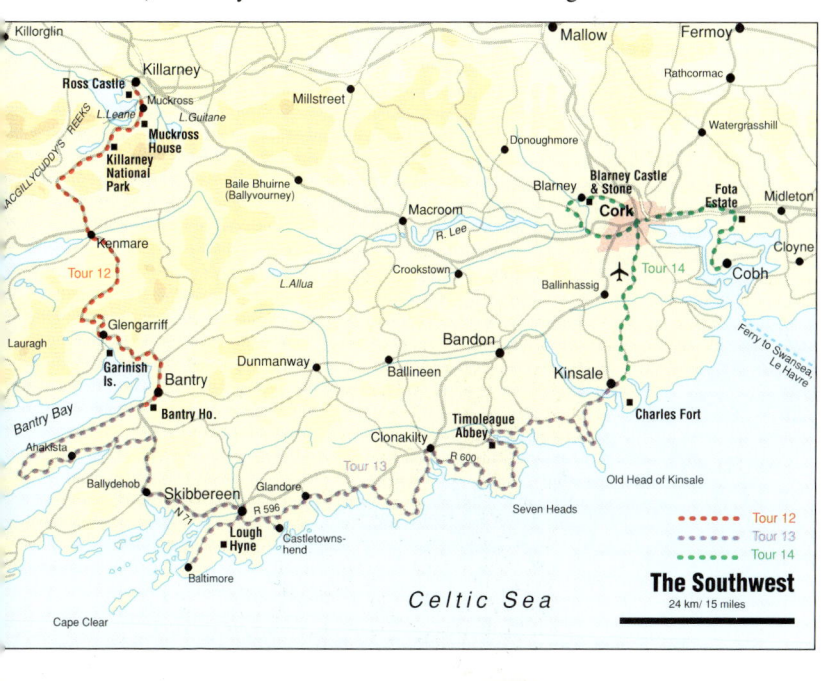

Muckross House

drinks and folk music in Buckley's Bar in College Street. South of the town, on the N22, sees the beginning of Killarney National Park and the Muckross Estates. If you want to see the estate in style, hire a jaunting car from the first entrance to the estate. Whether on foot or in a carriage, the first stop should be **Muckross Abbey**, founded by a Franciscan order in 1448, where some of Ireland's greatest poets are buried. **Muckross House**, a short distance further on, was donated to the nation in 1929 by the American senator, Arthur Vincent. Although built in 1843, there has been a succession of grand manors where the present house stands. Inside, there are elegant reception rooms, a restaurant and a working Folk Museum (daily, 9am–6pm) where visitors can see yesterday's ways of bookbinding, basket-weaving, harness-making and shoe-cobbling.

Coupled with the art treasures of the house, this provides a fascinating day in itself, especially if you take a horse-drawn jaunting car ride. Costing around £25 for up to four persons, a spin in a carriage takes you first to Muckross Abbey and House, and then around the lakes, up the old mountain ways to **Torc Waterfall**. In spring, when the shrubs are in full flower and the arboretum is starting to burst into blossom, this is the way to see Muckross. Proceeding on to Kenmare along the N71, prepare for a magnificent scenic drive that be-

Jaunting car

Glengarriff islets

gins with walls of rhododendron hedging at Muckross, skirts the shores of Muckross Lake, then passes into a wild glen where scrub birches grow amongst lichened rocks. Next comes a high climb to **Ladies View** for a look back up the Killarney Valley. Ladies View received its name after Queen Victoria's visit in 1861. Finally comes a high saddle drive across bogland before the descent into **Kenmare**, a genteel estate town built in 1773.

This charming town, situated where the Roughty River meets the sea, once thrived on iron smelting, then became famous for lace and needlepoint. Its history obviously goes further back as you can see by the dolmen surrounded by a stone circle near the town centre. The holy well of St Fionan across the river, near the church, has a reputation for healing. Coming out of Kenmare, we climb away from the Sheen Valley. This is known as the 'Tunnel Road' as the route often clings to the mountainside where some massive rock formations have been bored through. The last is the longest and will need headlights to negotiate. Then comes a sweeping descent with a vista over the creeks, islands and inlets of Glengarriff and the vastness of Bantry Bay with the Sheep's Head Peninsula. On a fine day in **Glengarriff**, you will see on the azure-blue, motionless water in the islet-dotted creeks, boats like statues frozen to their moorings. If you are a garden lover, then make time for **Ilnacullin**, the 15-hectare (38-acre) garden on **Garinish Island**. This is reached by boat from the harbour and you may enjoy the antics of playful seals on the way. Ilnacullin is an exotic formal garden. Particularly enchanting is an ornate Italiante garden with lily pond and fairytale pavilions. The island, barren until the early 18th century, was landscaped by Harold Peto (high summer, 9.30am–6.30pm; March to October, 10am–4.30pm). The last sight, as we drive to the head of Bantry Bay, are the Falls of Donermarc, which do not seem so spectacular after what we have already seen.

Hotels and Restaurants

Eccles Hotel
Glengarriff, Co Cork
Tel: 027-63003. $$
A grand if slightly shabby seafront hotel which once welcomed Queen Victoria. It has a reasonably good seafood restaurant and an old-fashioned bar warmed by a log fire.

Bantry House
Bantry, Co Cork
Tel: 027-50047. $$
Superb historic house decorated with Aubusson tapestries and Sheraton furniture with a lovely garden and glorious views over Bantry Bay. There are only 10 rooms, with dinner (and concerts) available.

13. From Bantry to Kinsale

From Bantry this scenic journey to Kinsale takes the Goat's Path Trail around the Sheep's Head Peninsula before going to colourful Skibbereen and characterful Baltimore. Then we take the coastal drive to Kinsale via Timoleague Abbey. Kinsale makes a lovely base for exploring the area (itineraries 13 and 14).

Bantry is a delightful market town and port at the head of the bay of the same name. Bantry House (daily, 9am–6pm) is a superb mansion overlooking the bay. The tiered Italianate gardens are lovely while the restored sections of the house are both intimate and eccentric. Many treasures and *objets d'art* to enjoy, especially the tiled floors pillaged from Pompeii and the Marie Antoinette tapestries. Most enjoyable are the Italian-style gardens with boxed parterres, lawns and antique urns set above the bay.

It is worth lingering on in Bantry if the monthly market is being held; here you might find that gear box for the Model T Ford, amongst rusty tin openers, broken tools and other ticky-tack. On leaving Bantry southward you will find the signs directing you round the scenic **Goat's Path Trail**. This drive follows the cliff tops of the **Sheep's Head Peninsula** with views across the bay to the backdrop of the Caha Mountains on the Beara Peninsula. In autumn the ankle-high dwarf furze gleams pure gold against the dying brown heather blooms.

Bantry House gardens

The return journey on the peninsula's south side at sea level offers a totally different coastline of low rocky promontories, with sheltered flat waters in the inlets. Just past the village of **Ahakista** is the memorial garden for all those lost in the sabotaged Air India 747 in 1985. At Durrus take the right-hand turn, then turn right again for **Skibbereen**, possibly the most colourful town in Ireland. Each building, whether shop or home, forms part of a complete rainbow of colour, mauve next to green alongside purple adjacent to yellow. There is none of your bland west-coast whitewash here! The buildings are like a string of Celtic jewels that jar, then delight the eye with agreeable surprise, especially on a drab rainy day. The West Cork Hotel, Bridge Street (Tel: 028-21277) is a good place for lunch where you will find home cooking served in vast quantities.

If you want more sophisticated pleasures, wait until you get to **Baltimore**, 13km (8 miles) southwest of Skibbereen, and try lobster or scallops at Chez Youen (Tel: 028-20136). Baltimore is a fishing and sailing centre with ferries to Cape Clear and Sherkin

Skibbereen

Island. In 1631 it was raided by Algerian pirates, who carried off some 200 villagers. Instead of heading directly back to Skibbereen, take the cross-country road some 6km (3¾ miles) to **Lough Hyne**, a marine nature reserve. This warm sea lake supports many Mediterranean-type species in its unique ecosystem. From here we proceed to **Castletownshend**, where Edith Somerville and Violet Martin – better known as Somerville and Ross, the co-authors of *Some Experiences of an Irish RM* (1899) – lived. They are buried in the Church of Ireland graveyard overlooking the coast.

Back on the R120, we turn off at Glandore, a sailing centre. Beyond is **Drombeg**, a stone circle dated to about the time of Christ. To the west of the circle are the remains of round huts, one of which contains a cooking trough where water was heated with hot stones and the food, wrapped in straw, was boiled. The R600 takes us through Rosscarbery and Clonakilty to the excellent ruins of the 14th-century Franciscan **Timoleague Abbey**. From here the road winds alongside the muddy estuary, with its plethora of wading birds, before turning inland to the tumbling fertile farmlands outside Kinsale. To round off the day, why not go out and back onto another peninsula. **The Old Head Of Kinsale** is attractive at any time, but especially at sunset. On 7 May 1915, some 25km (15 1/2 miles) offshore, the transatlantic liner *Lusitania* was torpedoed, and then sank with horrendous loss of civilian life. The sinking introduced the United States into the Great War of 1914–18. It is said that local people witnessed the event from the Old Head.

Timoleague Abbey

Hotels and Restaurants

BLUE HAVEN
3 Pearse Street, Kinsale, Co Cork
Tel: 021-772209. $$$
Outstanding seafood served in a charming setting, with a conservatory and garden.

SCILLY HOUSE
Scilly, Kinsale, Co Cork
Tel: 021-772413. $$
Friendly and beautifully sited hotel decorated with American colonial antiques. There are only six rooms, so book ahead.

COTTAGE LOFT
6 Main Street, Kinsale, Co Cork
Tel: 021-772803. $$
Gourmet cuisine from a gifted local owner/chef. Seafood in a low-key but charming setting. (Guest house accommodation)

KIERAN'S FOLKHOUSE INN
Guardwell, Kinsale, Co Cor
Tel: 021-772382. $/$$
Snug seafaring inn, with a small hotel, cosy bars and a restaurant with inventive dishes.

14. Kinsale and County Cork

A day's itinerary circling Cork, starting in Kinsale, (the 'gourmet capital' of Ireland), including kissing the Blarney Stone plus touring the arboretum at Fota and the port of Cobh.

Kinsale has a certain sniffy gentility and is really too picturesque for words, yet much has happened here that has influenced the history of Ireland. Kinsale saw the defeat of the Celtic chiefs in 1601. Another milestone was the execution of the English King Charles I, whose son, later to become Charles II, was crowned in St Multose Church 'with all the dignity the church could muster'. It was from Kinsale, after the Treaty of Limerick, that the banishment of the 'Wild Geese' began. This event meant the exile of all the Irish chiefs, many of whom went to fight for the armies of France and Spain. A few became known as 'wine geese' because they took to grape-growing in Cognac, Bordeaux and Burgundy. Today their names are known across the world: Hennessey, Delamain, Galway, Laughton, Barton, Dillon, etc. Now, generations later, their descendants return to Kinsale to be fêted for their vintages. Kinsale is definitely the right size for meandering around, with its harbour and yachting marina for colour, its forts, enchanting narrow streets and almshouses. It was the port from which the buccaneer Alexander Selkirk sailed on the epic voyages that left him stranded on a desert island. Later he was to meet Daniel Defoe and it was from his true story that *Robinson Crusoe* originated.

This, and other aspects of the town's history, are covered by the town's

Kinsale town

Museum (Monday to Saturday, 11am–5pm; Sunday, 3–5pm), once the Market House and built in the Dutch style in 1599. The displays are a curious hotchpotch of eccentric items, like the boots, knife and fork of Patrick O'Brien, the 2.52m (8ft 3in) tall giant, who died in 1802. Guardwell, nearby, is a quaint, narrow street, dotted with good restaurants and pubs.

After a coffee stop at Kieran's Folkhouse Inn, stroll around the corner to St Multose Church. This appealing church contains a Romanesque doorway and tower with the town stocks on display in the porch.

Charles Fort (mid-September to mid-June, Tuesday to Saturday, 9.30am–4.30pm, Sunday, 11am–5.30pm; mid-June to mid-September, daily, 9am–6pm) is the massive star-shaped fortress constructed in 1680 to the southeast of the town, the largest in Ireland. It is well worth a visit, having survived the siege of 1690. Considered the best-preserved fort in the country, Charles Fort overlooks Kinsale harbour and the ruins of **James Fort**, an earlier construction, marooned on a tongue of land. After Charles Fort, enjoy a well-deserved lunch in Kinsale, a leisurely and memorable gourmet experience.

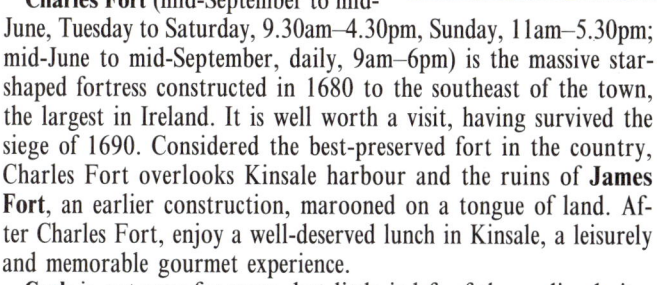

Cork is not very far away, but little is left of the medieval city. Even the cathedral of St Finbar is Victorian-Gothic. Let us instead, proceed around the city to **Blarney Castle** (daily, 9am–6pm or later) and kiss the stone for the 'eloquence that will come into our tongues'. There is an entrance fee, but it is, perhaps, more important to 'tip' Mr Dennis McCarthy, who sits atop the roof supporting people who want to kiss the stone. This is done by lying down, tilting the head backward over the castle wall whilst being held securely by Dennis. He handles some 150,000 kissers a year! Kissing the Blarney Stone is both a scary and exhilirating experience.

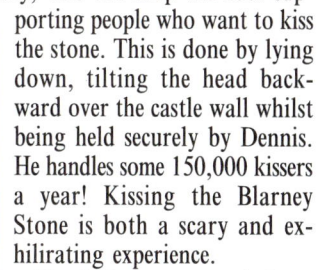

The 15th-century castle is essentially a traditional tower house surrounded by an atmospheric 'Druidic' dell and rock garden. The village and its green, despite all the hordes of tourists, still has immense appeal. Shopping here is a seri-

Kinsale harbour

ous activity, as this is the home of the **Blarney Woollen Mills** and the town has the greatest concentration of craft shops in the whole of Ireland.

For something more soothing drive back towards Cork, then eastward on the N25 for some 10km (6¼ miles) until the right turn for **Fota Estate**, **Arboretum** and **Wildlife Park** (April to October, Monday to Saturday, 10am–6pm; Sunday, 11am–6pm). The former was developed over 200 years ago by the Smith-Barry family. There are over 1,000 species of shrubs and trees set in 32ha (82 acres), each labelled with botanic and English names with their dates of planting. Despite public protest, the intriguing Fota House is closed, destined to become a club.

Turning right out of Fota we cross a delightful stone bridge where there is a castle tower on the left. For the next 6km (3¾ miles) the roadside scenery, sad to say, is an ecological disaster, consisting mainly of petrochemical plants. But this is the road to **Cobh** (pronounced 'cove').

I do hope your watch will say 5.45pm, in which case you will be in time to enjoy the 42-bell carillon, the largest in the British Isles, playing praises after the 6pm Angelus from the spiky-spired St Colman's Cathedral.

Cobh's past belongs with the sea and the Atlantic. It is home base for the world's oldest yacht club, founded in 1720, The Royal Cork. In its great days it saw all the famous Atlantic liners with the grandeur of their upper-deck life and the terrible tears of the famine-ravished, steerage emigrants. The major attraction in Cobh is the **Queenstown Story** (open daily, 9am–6pm), which is located within Cobh station.

This multi-media exhibition tells the story of a seafaring past and the suffering caused by Irish emigration. Since Cobh was the last port of call for the *Titanic*, a number of exhibits refer to the tragedy of the 'unsinkable' liner. The churchyard holds many of the nearly 2,000 victims of the *Lusitania*, sunk in dubious circumstances by a submarine.

The *Lusitania*'s victims are commemorated by a statue on the seafront before an empty harbour where once as many as 400 ocean-going vessels waited at their moorings.

Hotels and Restaurants

ARBUTUS LODGE
Montenotte, Cork, Co Cork
Tel: 021-501237. $$
Atmospheric late 18th-century hotel with a Michelin-starred restaurant; superb, inventive seafood dishes are the speciality but you can also lunch inexpensively in the Gallery Bar.

CLIFFORD'S
Dyke Parade, Cork, Co Cork
Tel: 021-275333. $$$
Situated in a converted library, this distinguished restaurant serves original Irish dishes. Expect the best of local cuisine, carefully and attractively presented

Kinsale Museum

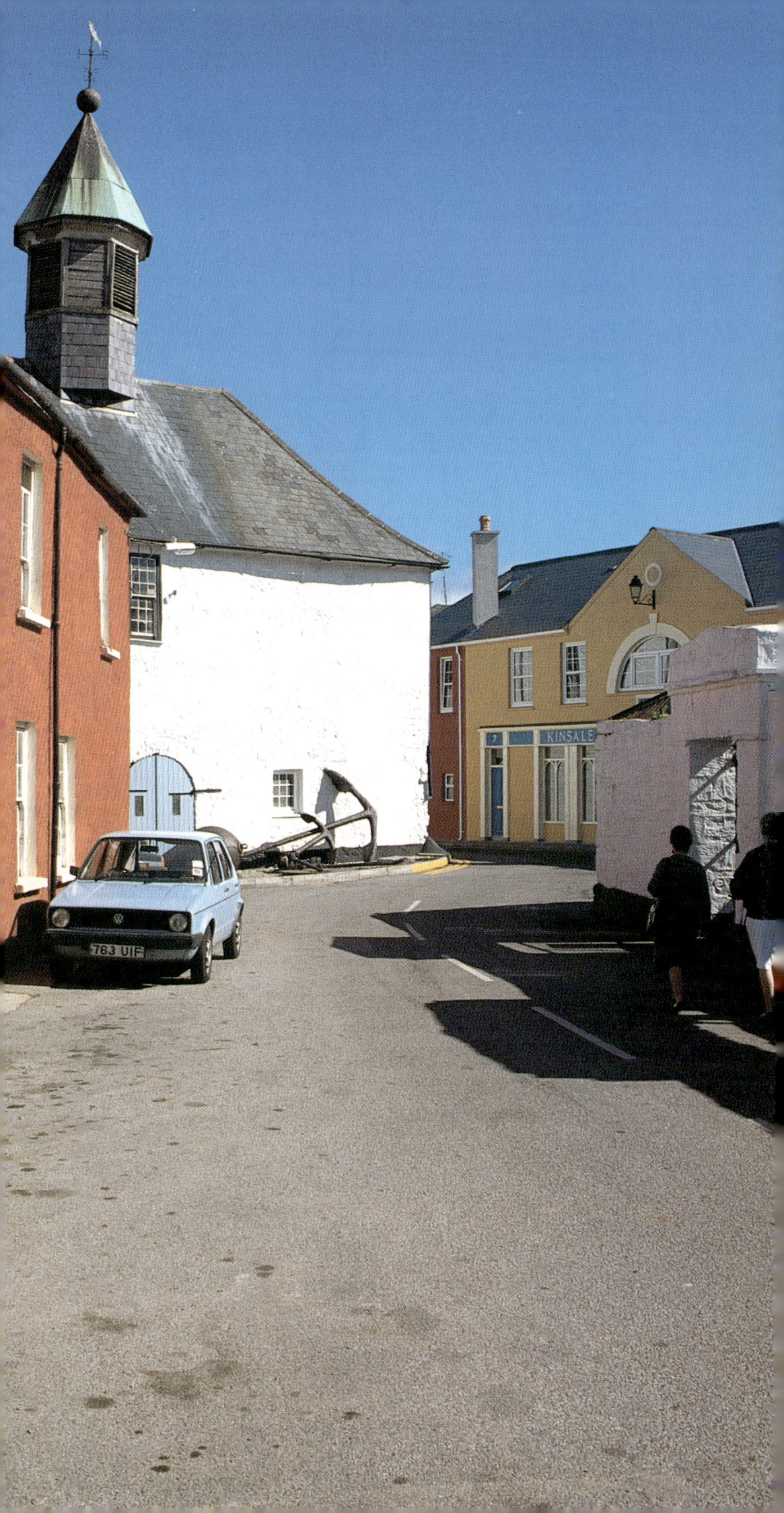
7
KINSALE
763 UIF

The Southeast

15. Cork to Waterford

A countryside, and latterly a coastal, drive from Cork to Waterford taking in Mallow, the woods and vales in the Blackwater Valley, the gardens of Anne's Grove, the Labbacallee megalithic passage tomb, Glanworth, Fermoy and Lismore with its lordly castle beneath the Knockmealdown Mountains, then on to Youghal, Dungarvan and finally to Waterford.

From Cork we go north to Mallow where you may choose to stop at **Mallow Castle** to see the herd of white deer, some of which may well be descendants of the bucks given by England's first Queen Elizabeth. Our main objective, however, lies beside the N72 eastwards towards Fermoy and we must turn right just before the main street in Mallow. Some 12km (7½ miles) out of Mallow we will be at **Anne's Grove**, a Georgian country manor at Castletownroche. This well-proportioned house has a frontage covered by mature climbing kiwi fruit. Today it is the home of Mr and Mrs Patrick Annesley, descendants of the garden's creator, and was 'something of an unexpected inheritance'. There are a dozen gardens based on one of three themes – woodland, formal and river – where exotic plants are blended informally with natives.

The Southeast I
24 km / 15 miles

'Baile' means settlement

From Anne's Grove we could take country roads across to **Glanworth** but that would mean missing **Bridgetown Abbey**, a turning to the right some 3km (1¼ miles) from Castletownroche back on the N72. This Augustinian priory, in its tranquil river setting, is much in need of basic repair and notices warn of crumbling masonry. Returning onto the N72 we make a left turn, at a village with the roisterous sounding name of **Ballyhooly**, to **Glanworth**. Here is Ireland's oldest stone bridge, built in 1600, with the ruins of the 13th-century Roche Castle towering up over the river. Coupled with a restored watermill and the ruins of a Dominican friary, we have a film set where the only missing elements are the actors. Some 3km (1¼ miles) to the south of the village is the **Labbacallee** wedge tomb. Finds here included early Bronze Age material and pottery. On the way we pass the fine, but broken, tower of Teampall Lobhair.

Fermoy, which we will soon reach but not enter, is a market town straddling the River Blackwater. The salmon ladder at the bridge always attracts a crowd of gazers after a good rainstorm to see the fish leaping their way upstream. We turn left before the bridge, following the R666 along the Blackwater's north bank, through woods and meadows with pastures sloping gently away. A few kilometres before we reach Lismore is a pull-in with a sign saying 'Towers'. Here is an opportunity to stretch our legs on a 20-minute round trip across a field or two. The sight we have come to see consists of two flamboyant gatehouses sitting bizarrely in the middle of nowhere. The story goes that a lady, trying to outdo her wealthy in-laws, plagued her husband for the grandest house. He was bankrupted having built just the servants' lodges.

The Labbacallee wedge tomb

Lismore, dominated by the massive castle of the Duke of Devonshire, had, from the 7th century, one of the most renowned universities in Europe, founded by St Carthach (also known as St Cartach or even St Carthage). This scholarly city was sacked, pillaged and plundered some 17 times over 600 years. It reached its height under St Colman in the 10th century with some 20 sites of learning. Today more mystery remains than fact. The medieval-looking castle (grounds open May to September, Sunday to Friday, 1.45–4.45pm) has very little originality having been built in 1814, but it must rate as the most romantic looking in all Ireland.

73

Youghal clock tower

We continue to **Cappoquin**, a market town and centre for sport fishing, then turn right and southwards towards the town of **Youghal** ('yawl') by the wooded and deep-cut Blackwater gorge. This historic seaport has an unusual clock tower that doubles as a gatehouse (1777). From the clocktower, stroll down North Man Street to see a cluster of historic buildings. On the left is the Red House, a gabled Dutch affair and, nextdoor, battered Elizabethan almshouses. Just left in William Street, visit Myrtle Grove, a delightful Tudor manor reputedly once owned by Sir Walter Raleigh. It was here that the film *Moby Dick*, starring Gregory Peck, was made and many stills from the movie are displayed in the quayside pub. Sir Walter Raleigh owned estates here for a short time. Whether it was here, or at Matrix Castle in Limerick, that the potato was first grown, who is to say? From Youghal we head east on the N25 to **Dungarvan** with its ruined castle merged into the remains of the old barracks. Just north of the town, at the junction for Cappoquin and Clonmel, is a monument to Master McGrath, a champion greyhound. Beaten only once in his career, he won the Waterloo Cup three times between 1868 and 1871. Finally we head onwards to **Tramore** on the R675, one of Ireland's most popular seaside resorts, with miles of sandy beaches, and on to **Waterford** city itself. Like neighbouring Wexford, Waterford is a Viking town and sections of the city walls remain from then. The most intriguing site is the newly renovated **Reginald's Tower**, the city's key Viking fortification.

Hotels and Restaurants

MOLANA RESTAURANT
Devonshire Arms Hotel
Pearse Square, Youghal, Co. Cork
Tel: 024-92827. $$$
Classic gourmet cuisine.

THE GRANVILLE
Meagher Quay
Waterford, Co Waterford
Tel: 051-55111. $$
Traditional but sombre hotel with good restaurant and central location.

WATERFORD CASTLE
The Island
Ballinakill, Co Waterford
Tel: 051-78203. $$$
This Fitzgerald family castle, built in the 17th century, stands on an island reached by ferry just outside Waterford. Four-poster beds and a strong sense of history are complemented by a good restaurant serving traditional Irish food. There are full sports facilities, including horse riding and fishing.

16. Cashel and Kilkenny

This circular day-long itinerary takes us from Waterford to the religious complex of the Rock of Cashel, once the seat of the Munster Kings, and to the prosperous medieval town of Kilkenny. It is a day spent exploring fabled ecclesiastical wonders, depicting the wealth and power of the pre-Reformation Church, and for enjoying some of Ireland's most stately castles.

Kilkenny

From Waterford we take the N24 and drive the 27km (16¾ miles) to **Carrick on Suir**, situated on one of the prettiest stretches of the Suir River. The Manor House, which is built into the castle, is said to be the birthplace of Ann Boleyn (open June to September). Some 10km (6¼ miles) to the north of the town are the high crosses at Ahenny, worth the drive if you are interested in Celtic sculpture. Otherwise we continue towards Clonmel, the nation's centre for greyhound racing, perhaps stopping at the small factory shop of **Tipperary Crystal** on the outskirts of the town on the N24 to Cahir. **Cahir** (pronounced 'care') has a magnificent castle surrounded by flour mills on the banks of the Suir, (daily, 10am–7.30pm). This well-restored stronghold dates back to the 13th century. After admiring the three wards, clamber along the battlements for a good view.

Our main aim for this part of the day is the **Rock of Cashel** (daily May to September, 9am–7.30pm; October to April, 9.30am–

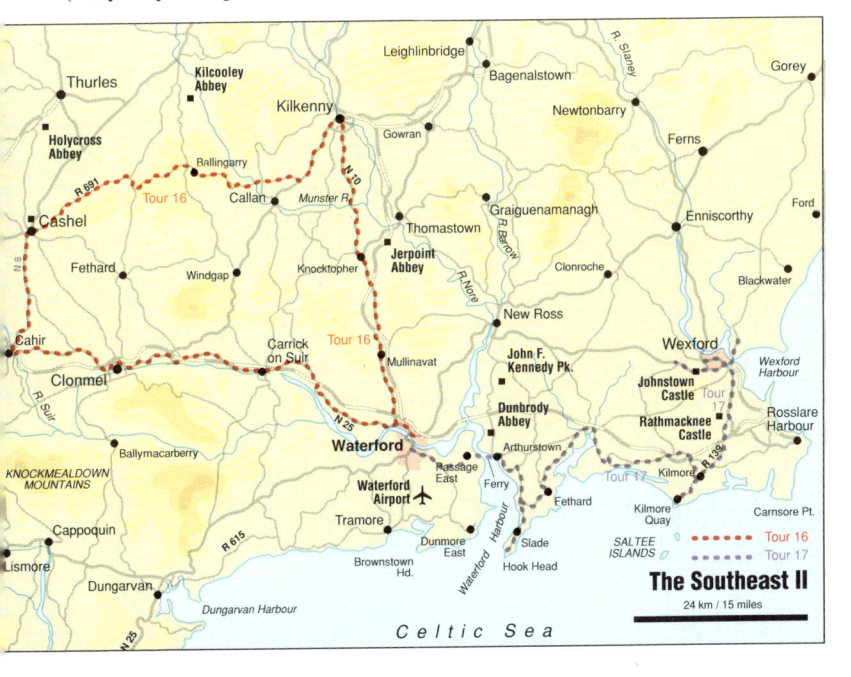

4.30pm). Take the N8 from Cahir northbound for some 18km (11¼ miles) and it cannot be missed. The town hall is worth visiting for its museum and there are interesting craft shops. But it is the majesty of the cluster crowning the 63m (206ft) limestone outcrop, rising from the Tipperary Plain that has drawn us here today. This was once the seat of the Munster Kings, until it was granted to the Church in 1101. Entrance is via the Hall of the Vicars Choral, the only isolated structure. The Round Tower is thought to date from the 12th century; the 14th-century cathedral is now roofless.

The gem is **Cormac's Chapel**, built in the Romanesque style, considered one of Europe's finest chapels and begun in 1127. It is strangely sited alongside the cathedral, but askew of due east to meet the sunrise on St Cormac's day. The stone beneath the high cross is thought to be the one upon which the ancient kings were crowned. The entire complex was eventually abandoned in the middle of the 18th century. From the rock, if you are a view addict, let the eye wander across Tipperary's sweeping grasslands. To the southwest is the far-off grandeur of the Galtees; to the south lie the Knockmealdowns and to the southeast the Comeraghs.

From this literal high spot we drive straight to Kilkenny on the R691, joining the N76 for the final 11km (6¾ miles). **Kilkenny** is a city that has thrived for more than 1,000 years. It remains extremely prosperous and little changed. The place to start is the **Shee Almshouse** (Rose Inn Street; Monday to Saturday, 9am–5.15pm), built by a Tudor benefactor, which is also the home of the tourist office. Upstairs is an imaginative audio-visual presentation using a computer-controlled illuminated model of the city as it was in the 17th century. Not only does it help you get to grips with the town's history, it will also enable you to walk out, completely orientated, to enjoy the city's many offerings.

Craftsman at Tipperary Crystal

Still dominating the city is the stately **castle** (daily, 10am–7pm; Sunday, 11am–5pm), seat of the Butler family, the Dukes of Ormond, set in rich parklands. Built in the 13th century, it has been altered through time but is now splendidly restored. A walk from the castle into the High Street would bring us to the arcaded 18th-century

St Canice's Cathedral

Tholsel or **Town Hall**. Further on is **Rothe House** (Monday to Saturday, 10.30am–5pm; Sunday, 3–5pm), a Tudor merchant's house, now the headquarters of the archaeological society with fine courtyards and a Costume Museum. Still walking along the High Street, you can turn left into Blackmill Street for **Black Abbey**, an over-restored Dominican abbey, and on to **St Canice's Cathedral** (Monday to Saturday, 9am–6pm; Sunday, 2–6pm). The cathedral dates from 1285 and has fine medieval monuments, effigies, altar tombs and other sculptures.

If you enjoy shopping for Irish goods – such as linen, pewter, whiskey, knitwear, glass and crystal – then visit the celebrated **Kilkenny Design Centre**, set in the castle stables.

You may be so enamoured of Kilkenny that you choose to stay the night here and continue exploring tomorrow. If so, be sure to book a short walking tour of the town at the tourist office. Otherwise our route back to Waterford takes us first on the R697 southward to Kells, not to be confused with the other Kells, in County Meath, where the famous book was illuminated.

The first sight of **Kells** from afar is one of the great surprises of Ireland. It seems we behold not a religious centre but a mighty battlemented citadel with towers as awesome as the Rock of Cashel. The massive walls hide 2ha (5 acres) of ruined priory. Our final destination is **Jerpoint Abbey** (daily, 9.30am–6pm), which lies east, beyond Stonyford.

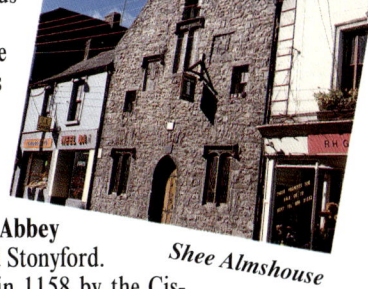

Shee Almshouse

Do not miss this abbey. It was founded in 1158 by the Cistercians and is one of the finest and mightiest of monastic ruins in Ireland. Here, amongst the cloisters, the quadrangle and the three-naved church with its Romanesque arches, you can easily picture the might of the Church in its heyday. Turning left from Jerpoint we join the N9 southbound and, in just over 30 minutes, return to Waterford.

Hotels and Restaurants

BLANCHVILLE HOUSE
Dunbell, Maddoxtown
Tel: 056-27197. $
Warm hospitality in a period country house 10 miles from Kilkenny.

RINUCCINI RESTAURANT
The Parade, Kilkenny City
Tel: 056-61575. $$
Irish and Italian cuisine in the city's best restaurant.

Slade harbour

17. Waterford to Wexford

Today starts with an appreciation of Waterford city, then a scenic coastal drive to Hook Head and the oldest lighthouse in Europe. Via the enchanting anchorage at Slade, Tintern Abbey ruins and Kilmore Quay, we visit the Irish National Heritage Park at Ferrycarrig before arriving in Wexford.

Hearing the name **Waterford**, do you think of a Viking city founded in AD853 or of lead crystal? Make time for both. The crystal factory is at **Kilbarry** to the southeast of the centre. The city, at the mouth of the River Suir, enjoys two cathedrals and has played a major role in history. Founded by the Danes, it was the first stronghold that fell to the Anglo-Norman invasion of 1170, an event that would slowly break up old Celtic Ireland and bring about 700 years of turmoil and agony. Worth seeing is Reginald's Tower built in 1003, part of the Danish defences, the old city walls, founded in the 9th century and strengthened in medieval times, and the cathedrals of Christ Church and Holy Trinity.

Departing from Waterford, take the well-signed road to **Passage East** to cross the swift-running estuary of Waterford Harbour by ferry. It was here that the Norman invader, Strongbow, landed with his fighting force in 1170 to be joined a year later by Henry II of England. The ferry runs every 15 minutes (up to 8pm in winter, 10pm in summer). The ferry delivers us at **Arthurstown** with its anchorages for small fishing boats. Nearby is Dunbrody Park, the family seat of the Marquess of Donegal, and a little further north is the **John F Kennedy National Park** created as a memorial since the family orig-

Waterford

inally came from nearby Dunganstown (daily, May to August, 10am–8pm; March to April and September to October, 10am–5pm). The park's highlight is the arboretum where thousands of trees, given by all nations, cover the slopes of Slieve Caoilte, once a rebel battle camp in 1798. On the way back to Arthurstown, follow the signs to **Ballyhack**, a quaint village, for lunch at the Neptune Restaurant (Tel: 051-89284) specialising in seafood.

Back in Arthurstown, follow the east side of Waterford Harbour until the road points us inland, then turn right to pick up the road signs for Hook Head. For the next 16km (10 miles) our drive offers fine coastal views across the broad estuary. At **Hook Head** the lighthouse is reputedly the oldest surviving in Europe, going back 1,200 years. Beneath its bulky Norman tower are cells once lived in by monks who manned the early beacon. Although there are notices forbidding entry, you can, in fact, knock on the door and ask permission to view. For far more spectacular views cross the pencil-thin peninsula to **Slade**, a detour of less than 2km (1¼ miles) before returning. Just go straight on and do not turn left. This must be the most enchanting fishing harbour in all of Ireland, from which rises a deserted castle built by the Laffan family in the 17th century. The key is available from the caretaker whose address is posted on the castle door.

We return on the same road that came up the peninsula, but turn right to **Fethard**, a busy summer resort, with Baginbun Head where Strongbow's scouting force landed. The area

Picture Window

around Fethard is rich in early church and castle ruins. Some 8km (5 miles) further along is the awesome Cistercian **Tintern Abbey**, founded by William the Earl Marshall in 1200 to honour his vow of thanks for surviving a stormy crossing from England after his boat beached in the nearby creek. Currently the building is under restoration. Turn right off the R734 and take the R733 to Wellington Bridge. Looking south from the bridge a castle can be seen amongst the ruins of **Clonmines**, a silver mining town that died in the 17th century after the river silted up. Our next stop is **Kilmore Quay**, famous for its thatched cottages, some 20km (12½ miles) down the R736. Kilmore Quay is the departure point for boat outings to the bird sanctuaries on the Saltee Islands. Sadly, the thatched cottages are drowning amongst modern developments.

Next we turn inland to **Kilmore**. On the far side of the village, just before the cemetery on the right, is a hawthorn tree. Amongst the branches are piles of funeral crosses. Following ancient custom, two funeral crosses accompany the deceased and one is placed in the tree. The origin of this strange practice is unclear. Some 6km (3¾ miles) north of Kilmore you can turn right onto the R736 and seek out the Tacumshin Windmill, or continue towards Wexford on the R739. To the left will be signed **Rathmacknee Castle**, seat of the Rossiter family and now a ruin. You can get the key from the family that lives within the castle precincts. Take care if walking around the roof; no guard rails exist. Perhaps the best reason for visiting is to meet the family, who have a castle surrounding their home. County Wexford has many examples of homes sprouting from within castle ruins.

Proceed not into Wexford but on, via the bypass, to **Johnstown Castle** (weekdays, 9am–5pm; weekends, 2–5pm), a Gothic Revival fantasy that is now an agricultural college with museum, mature shrub gardens, arboretum and ornamental lakes. On leaving, turn left and follow the signs for **The Irish National Heritage Park** at Ferrycarrig (daily, 9am–7pm March to October). This is an interesting and well-thought-out project, which portrays human evolution from 8000BC to the 12th century. Accurate reconstructions have been made by archaeologists, based on information from excavated sites. The tableaux, which you can either explore independently or with a guide (1½ hours), will tell you all about dolmens, stone circles, ring forts, Celtic villages and vanished lifestyles.

Wexford harbour

Finally we reach **Wexford**, home of Commodore John Barry, founder of the US Navy. The streets are so amazingly narrow that parking is nigh impossible. This is the end point of our journey round Ireland's coast. As a last reminder of all that is wild and beautiful about Ireland, I recommend that you head out at sunset across the harbour bridge and take the road to North Slob. This road leads to the **Wildfowl Protection Area** where innumerable birds gather, mainly Greenland white-fronted geese. At certain times, especially evenings during the winter months, they take off *en masse* and darken the sky, creating an awesome sight, which can best be enjoyed from the observation tower.

Hotels

THE TALBOT HOTEL
Trinity Street, Wexford, Co Wexford
Tel: 053-22566. $$
Lively, comfortable hotel. Inexpensive restaurant, pool, squash courts.

NEWBAY HOUSE
County Wexford
Tel: 053-42779. $$
Elegant family-run Georgian mansion 3 kms (2 miles) from Wexford town.

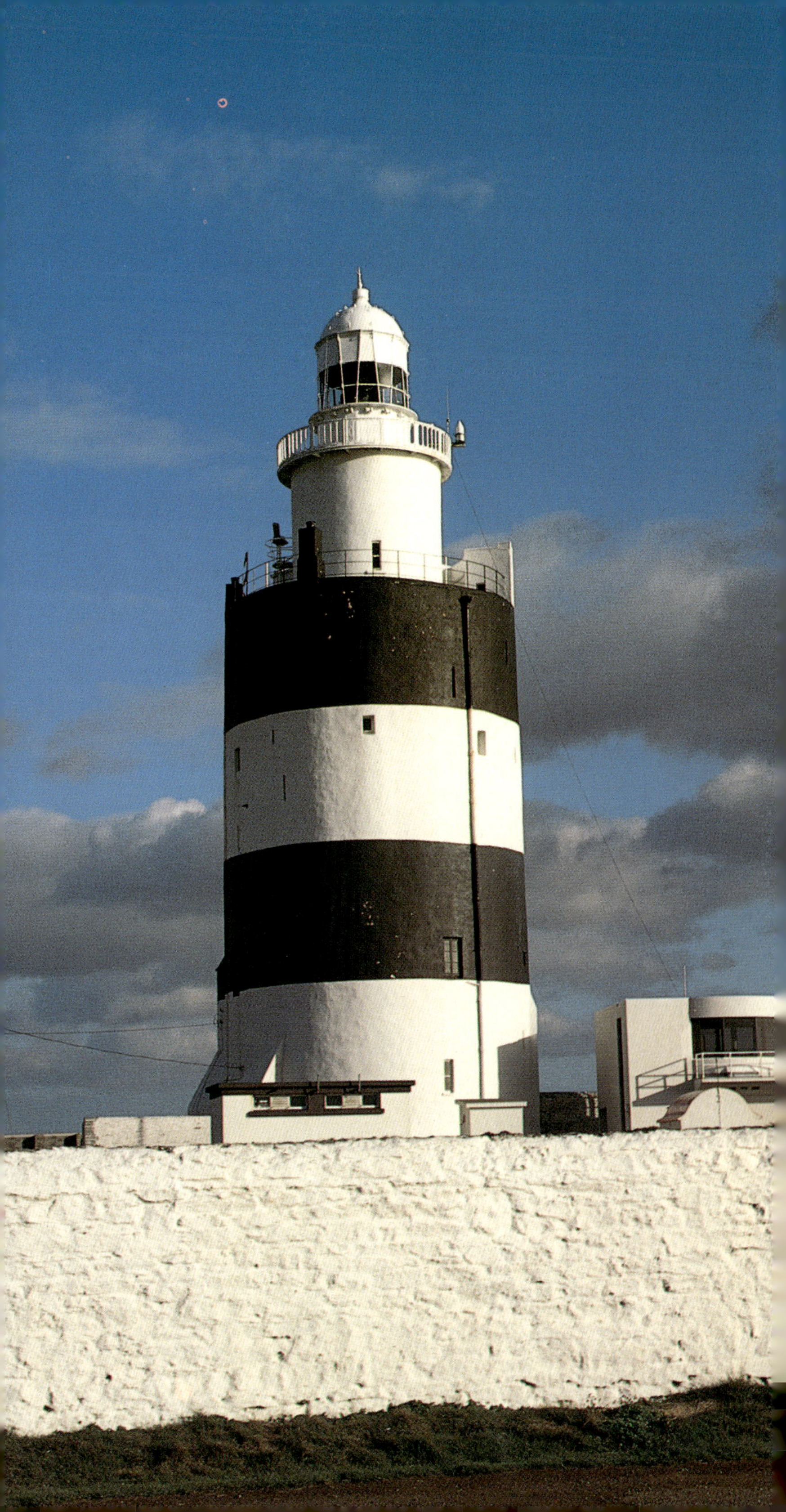

Shopping

Dublin

The first rule of the shopper says 'start at the top of the hill when empty-handed'. **Grafton Street**, Dublin's main shopping thoroughfare, is on an incline rising from College Green, so starting at the **St Stephen's Green Shopping Centre** at the top of Grafton Street would seem sensible. In this comfortable Victorian setting are some 75 shops ranging from fashion and designer wear to Irish crafts. The sweeter-toothed might prefer to start at **Butler's Handmade Chocolate** shop right opposite.

Some 50m (150ft) down Grafton Street turn left towards the **Powerscourt Townhouse** complex. It occupies the courtyard of a restored Georgian town house and offers entertainment and live music, antiques, Irish handmade goods including Celtic jewellery, crystal and designer clothes. For the best of Irish fashion visit the **Design Centre** to choose clothes by Louise Kennedy and Mariad Whisker. Nearby is the **Craft Council of Ireland**, with quality pottery, fabrics and baskets. If peckish, pop into **Chompeys**, an American deli, or **Blazing Saddles**, a vegetarian restaurant.

Shopping in Dublin

Before returning to Grafton Street look for the **Irish Cheese Board** shop for farmhouse cheeses and **Magill's Deli** on nearby Clarendon Street, which sells all manner of Irish produce such as preserves, jams, honey, smoked foods and cheeses. Back on Grafton Street visit **A-Wear**, a fashion store selling cut-price designer clothes, including John Rocha and Quin and Donnelly collections. At the lower end of Grafton Street are **Switzer's** and **Arnott's** department stores offering leading fashions. If you need a break, try stopping in for coffee at **Bewley's Oriental Café**, halfway up Grafton Street, whose coffee-roasting aromas attract everyone who passes by. Since 1840 the mahogany-panelled rooms have wrapped themselves around politicians, students, poets and artists who mingle with out-of-town shoppers. Before leaving buy coffee or chocolates to take home.

Turning right into busy Nassau Street you will find speciality shops for Donegal tweeds, Aran sweaters, Royal Tara chinaware and Irish pewter. The first call is at **Blarney Woollen Mills** shop offering quality Irish woollens and knits. Almost next door is the **Kilkenny Shop** presenting an array of Irish arts and crafts including fabrics, candles, pottery, glass and woodwork. Equally fascinating is the cluster of long-established **bookshops**, especially Fred Hanna. If you have Irish family connections, the genealogy shop of **Heraldic Artists** is the place to trace your lineage and buy items decorated with your family coat of arms.

In Pearse Street, the other side of Trinity College, is the **Tower Design Craft Centre**. This historic building of the 1860s has 30 traditional artists working on site in ceramics, tiles, heraldic jewellery, gold, silver, handpainted silks and woodwork items made from aged, carbon-dated bog-oak. There is a restaurant on the first floor.

If you are looking for the offbeat in art or antiquities or for fishing tackle, you should explore **Thomas Street** beyond Christchurch Cathedral, a rather seedy area, but rewarding. For 'alternative' gifts, shop in the vibrant Temple Bar quarter.

No shopping spree would be complete without a visit to **Moore Street Market** behind the General Post Office on O'Connell Street. Prepare to be astonished, not just by the characters, the noise, the array of goods (anything from fireworks to used newspapers) but also by the hundreds of prams belonging to illegal traders, who can 'leg a quick getaway' at the very rumour of the 'boys in blue'.

Rural Ireland

Driving from town to town you will find small craft centres, hardware stores and even family homes selling **traditional loom-woven tweeds**. Many outlets have hand-written signs, but even in the middle of nowhere you can often find that 'special something', particularly in the west and south. All **country market towns** have excellent shops offering linens, lace, plaids, books, prints, crystal, woodwork, ornaments and jewellery.

Left to right: The House of Ireland, Waterford Crystal and Kilkenny Design

Antiques

Though no longer the bargains they once were, Irish furniture, sterling silver items and Irish landscape paintings can still be found. In Dublin try the Francis Street area for antiques.

Pottery, Fine China and marble

Throughout Ireland studio pottery is thriving. The famous Belleek bone china is sold in all department stores. Connemara marble is sold everywhere.

Art

Dublin galleries are as adventurous as the new young artists. Fine traditional watercolour landscapes can be found across the land.

Crystal and Glassware

World-famous Waterford crystal is sold all over Ireland but crystal from Tipperary, Galway and Dublin are challenging the Waterford monopoly.

Weaves

Irish handwoven tweeds are renowned worldwide for their quality, design, versatility and colour blends. In the west, most tweeds are still woven on looms in the home. You can buy direct from the weaver or at sales centres such as Magee's in Donegal.

For the Home Bar and Larder

Whiskey (spelled with an 'e' to distinguish it from Scotch whisky) makes an excellent present. Smoked salmon, cheeses, bacon and conserves are also popular gifts. In Dublin visit the Irish Whiskey Corner (Bow Street, Smithfield. Tel: 01-8725566). Near Cork, visit the authentic Jameson distillery at Midleton (Tel: 021-613594). After trailing through the mills and mattings you get to sample the whiskey.

Handknits

Aran Island sweaters, scarves, caps, gloves, etc, are made from undyed wool to family patterns passed down generations. Donegal and nearby Ardara have the best range.

Jewellery

Celtic traditions live on, and craft centres stock items ranging from repro ancient Celtic gold, silver and enamel work to daring contemporary designs.

Linen and Lace

Look out for fine table coverings, furnishing fabrics, shirts and blouses as well as handkerchiefs.

Marble

Connemara marble and other colourful stone, fashioned into everything from bookends to cheeseboards, is on sale throughout the country.

Music

The recent popularity of Irish traditional music has resulted in the appearance of stores selling everything from recordings, music and song sheets to musical instruments.

St Columbs House Kitchen

Eating Out

Ireland is an agricultural country, and early mornings combined with long days of hard manual labour call for **substantial fare** to rekindle the inner fire. Irish food, traditionally, has been plain but hearty and plentiful. Bread, potatoes and root vegetables have served to eke out and soak up the meat and juices of stew cooked slowly in a tureen over an open peat fire. Such traditional fare is still to be found in the home and in rural hotel dining rooms, but a new generation of gifted chefs, have transformed the 'poor man's' food of Ireland into dishes fit for earls and kings.

Ireland is no longer a 'bacon and cabbage' cuisine but one reliant on quality produce, especially beef, lamb, farmhouse cheeses and Atlantic Coast fish and shellfish. **Irish stew**, for example, can be a heavy dish of mutton, potatoes and onions but, in the hands of a gifted chef who uses the best cuts of lamb and herb-fragrant stock, it can be a superbly light and flavoursome dish. In Dublin, Kinsale and Galway, in particular, you will find no shortage of gourmet experiences and at prices that compare very favourably to international standard cuisine elsewhere in the world. Country house hotels often provide excellent food in beautiful surroundings while pubs offer filling lunches.

The Shelbourne Hotel, Dublin

Breakfasts in Ireland are still hearty enough to fuel you for the day; expect a gargantuan plate of fried bacon, sausage, eggs and tomatoes as just one course of the first meal of the day, sometimes accompanied by black pudding and **savoury potato cakes**. If you indulge in breakfast to the full, you may only want a light lunch; most pubs in Ireland serve bar food ranging from simple sandwiches and salads to more substantial roasts and stews. *Boxties*, traditional stuffed pancakes, can be found on many a regional menu.

Travelling in the west of Ireland you will encounter numerous restaurants specialising in fish, freshly caught and of the highest quality. Lobsters, salmon, river trout and oysters are commonplace luxuries that make eating here both pleasurable and healthy. Mussels, crab and lobster are also popular. Do not be surprised if, among the traditional Irish bars and restaurants, you also find Chinese restaurants serving some of the best and most **authentic fish dishes** to be found outside Asia itself.

Game will also feature on the menu if you are travelling in the autumn and winter. Dishes of venison, pheasant, quail, duck, woodcock and rabbit are all likely to appear on the menu, along with the all-season staples such as steak, lamb and pork. Irish **beef and lamb** are considered amongst the best in the world, with east-coast lamb praised for its delicacy and Connemara lamb enjoyed for its intensity and herb flavourings.

Fresh from the fields and orchards

Outside cities and major tourist centres, there is still a tendency to **eat early**; until comparatively recently, lack of electricity for lighting in the rural areas meant that you went to bed with the sun. Outside the big cities, **dairy products** play an important role in Irish cuisine. Home-made or farm-fresh cheeses, such as Cashel Blue, a soft, creamy blue cheese, are fast becoming known.

Bread in most good restaurants tends to be delicious and home-made, with soda bread the most typical. Irish bread goes well with the simple farmhouse cheeses from the Midlands or County Cork. **Irish fruit** tends to be fairly limited but the quality of soft fruits, in particular, leaves little to be desired. County Wexford is usually considered the centre of the soft fruit industry and is noted for its magnificent strawberries. In short, the patronising view of Ireland as a centre of a 'bacon and cabbage' cuisine is no longer deserved. Restaurants will be busiest between 7.30pm and 8.30pm.

The ratings in the guide refer to a meal for two (with wine) in the appropriate price category below:

$$$ = Expensive (over £50)
$$ = Moderate (£30–£50)
$ = Inexpensive (under £30).

Nightlife

The Dublin pub has a long tradition of being the informal meeting ground of mind with mind, the exchange of wit and humour and the sanctuary of dialogue. Although many of the old bars have changed their décor, there are still those that keep alive the ghosts of Dublin's past. The way to visit them is by selecting an area that has pubs of special character after first having a 'ritual' drink in the **Horseshoe Bar** in the **Shelbourne Hotel** on St Stephen's Green.

Less than a minute's walk from St Stephen's Green, on Lower Baggott Street, is **O'Donoghue's**, famous for its folk music and the place where *The Dubliners* first began their career. Hardly a minute beyond is **Doheny and Nesbitt** with its confessional 'snug' set around a mahogany bar below a smoke encrusted ceiling; a favourite haunt of writers, raconteurs and journalists. Almost opposite is **Toner's**, dating back to the early 19th century, with its wooden storage drawers.

Working your way up Grafton Street, sampling the bars, is an enjoyable way to spend the evening. Starting from the Nassau Street end of Grafton Street, the first stop on the left is **Kehoe's** in South Anne Street, with its finely carved confessional partitions. Next is the **Bailey** in Duke Street, where Gogarty is supposed to have introduced James Joyce to the pleasure of drink. It serves excellent roasts and oak-smoked salmon upstairs. Nearby in Duke Street is **Davy Byrne's** 'moral pub' featured in Joyce's *Ulysses* and noted for its good food. On the other side of Grafton Street is **Neary's** in Chatham Street, noticeable by its lanterns which indicate its Edwardian atmosphere.

Another group of characterful pubs is concentrated in the Trinity College

Tipping a glass of gold

area. At the **Oscar Wilde** in College Street students mingle with hacks from Dublin's press; **Bowes**, in Fleet Street, is all mirrors and mahogany. The **Palace Bar**, also in Fleet Street, is where hacks from the *Irish Times* gather to relax. For real native Dubliners **Mulligan's** in Poolbeg Street beats them all.

Theatres

Dublin has a long theatrical tradition stretching back all the way to Georgian times, though it was not until the turn of the century that Irish writers were able to break away from outside influences and find their own voice. Today Dublin's theatres play an important role in Irish cultural life

THE ABBEY THEATRE
Lower Abbey Street
Tel: 01-8787222
Regarded as Ireland's national theatre, founded by Yeats and Lady Gregory. Specialises in works by Irish playwrights.

THE GAIETY THEATRE
South King Street
Tel: 01-6771717
Productions more reflective of Broadway and London's West End. Also has two opera seasons.

THE GATE THEATRE
Parnell Square East
Tel: 01-8744045
Classic Irish productions mixed with European notables such as Ibsen and Chekov. Orson Welles made his first stage appearance here.

Traditional Music

Music lovers, throughout the world, are awakening to the intoxicating sounds of Irish traditional music with its insistent rhythms and flighty melodies. A gathering of musicians, always on an informal basis, is known as a *seisiún* and can be best compared to animated conversation, sometimes casual but often passionate. A good *seisiún* is to be experienced rather than described. Many of the best places for traditional music are within 10–15 minutes' walk of the city centre:

THE BRAZEN HEAD
20 Lower Bridge Street
Music and set dancing take place most nights of the week in the 'oldest bar in Dublin'.

HUGHES PUB
19 Chancery Street
Music from around 9pm nightly.

McDAIDS
Harry Street
Tel: 679 3797
Live music (including blues upstairs) in this pub off Grafton Street.

SLATTERY'S
129 Capel Street
Set dancing and balls as well as blues, folk and jazz.

IRISH TRADITIONAL MUSIC ARCHIVE
63 Merton Square South
Tel: 01-872 2077
A repository of traditional music – open to the public.

Impromptu music in a Dublin pub

The Nightclub Scene

Dublin is a hive of nocturnal activity and has an immensely lively club scene, catering for every shape and size of night-owl. Most of the clubs are situated close to the city centre and provide a range of haunts for the trendy to the sophisticated. As a rule the club scene is divided into two; fully licensed clubs serving a full range of drinks, with a cover charge of about £10, and wine-only clubs which have no cover fee. Both have strict door policies and expensive drinks. Generally a pint of lager will cost almost £5, with £20 being the average for a bottle of wine. To keep up with the nightclub scene, check venues in the bi-monthly *In Dublin* magazine

LILLIE'S BORDELLO
Adam Court (off Grafton Street)
Tel: 01-6799204
The most sought-after spot for supermodels and rock stars. This boudoir-style club is members only on Friday and Saturday.

THE KITCHEN
Clarence Hotel, Wellington Quay
Tel: 01-6776178
Trendy young club in U2's equally trendy hotel.

The Leeson Street Strip

'The Strip' consists of over a dozen small underground nightclubs which run the length of Leeson Street. They only serve wines and have no cover charge. These subterranean dens operate from midnight to dawn, and can be identified by the black-suited bounc-

Cheers

Paddy and his pint

There are several good regional theatres and cultural centres in the larger towns, such as Cork, Limerick, Galway, Wexford and Kilkenny. Several less well-known towns, including Tralee and Cashel, run reputable folk theatres. (In Tralee, contact the Siamese Tire Company; Tel: 066-23055). The Shannon Development Corporation's medieval banquets are well worth attending (Tel: 061-360788). Expect jesters, minstrels, folk dances, 'medieval' food – and lots of blarney.

However, the best nightlife is focused on the pubs, the place for Guinness, traditional music and *craic* (pronounced 'crack'). meaning fun and chat. Here are just a few of the typical and lively pubs; many others are mentioned in the itineraries.

ers outside. popular clubs are Annabels (Burlington Hotel, Upper Leeson Street, Tel: 01-6605222) and the more soul and blues-oriented Suesey Street (Lower Leeson Street).

POD
35 Old Harcourt Street
Tel: 01-4780166
Set in an old railway vault, the **Place of Dance** appeals to dance fanatics.

ROCK GARDEN
Crown Alley, Temple Bar
Tel: 01-6799114
This raunchy, loud, futuristic club hosts rock bands and serves American-style food.

Nightlife Ireland

'Impromptu' is the keyword for all nightlife in the country towns and villages of Ireland. An evening out usually means visiting a pub for live traditional music. There is no set programme – activities 'happen' as opposed to being planned. Ask at your hotel whether a *seisiún* is scheduled anywhere for that evening. If, by the way, you are a musician yourself, do take your instrument when you travel around Ireland.

KYTELERS
Kieren Street, Kilkenny, Co Kilkenny
This medieval inn was the house of Alice Kybeler who was accused of witchcraft and died in 1324. The cellar bar is darkly atmospheric.

DURTY NELLY'S
Bunratty, Co Limerick
This boisterous inn dates from 1620 and is a good warm-up to the banquet next door at Bunratty Castle.

REGINALD'S BAR
Reginald's Tower
Waterford, Co Waterford
Set beside the Viking bastion, this long established pub and restaurant adjoins ancient city wall, visible inside the pub.

1601
Pearce Street, Kinsale, Co Cork
This popular pub was named after the decisive Battle of Kinsale in 1601, which marked the end of the old Gaelic order. Inside, however, the Celtic spirit is very much alive, as is the *craic*.

Calendar of Special Events

JANUARY – FEBRUARY

Beginning of the point-to-point horse-racing season. Races are held all over Ireland, usually on a Sunday.

Punchestown Bloodstock Sales, Co Kildare, Ireland's foremost racehorse auction.

The Five Nations rugby season begins, with matches at Landsdowne Road, Dublin.

Dublin Film Festival, usually at the end of the month and into March.

MARCH – MAY

St Patrick's Day, 17 March; celebrations all over Ireland for the feast of the nation's patron saint; street parades in Dublin and traditional music festivals all over the country. Should the festival fall on a weekend, the following Monday is a holiday.

West of Ireland Golf Championships, Rosses Point, County Sligo.

The Irish Grand National at Fairyhouse, County Meath, during Easter.

International Choral and Folk Dance Festival, held in Cork.

County Wicklow Gardens Festival, with gardens and gourmet cuisine.

The Irish 2,000 Guineas horse-race, the Curragh, County Kildare.

Mussel Festival. This is held in Bantry in May.

Pilgrim on Mt Croagh Patrick

World Irish Dancing Championship. This takes place in Dublin in March.

JUNE – AUGUST

Bloomsday Literary Festival, on 16 June, is a celebration of the author James Joyce staged in Dublin with a pilgrimage around the city visiting all the places mentioned in *Ulysses*, as well as readings from the writer's landmark novel.

Bathmullen Fishing Festival. This takes place in County Donegal in June.

The Festival of Music in Great Irish Houses, classical concerts in stately homes around Dublin.

The Irish Derby, takes place in the Curragh, County Kildare.

The Galway Oyster Festival

SEPTEMBER – OCTOBER

Oyster festivals are held in Galway and Clarinbridge.

Hurling and Gaelic football finals at Croke Park, Dublin.

Match-Making Festival in Lisdoonvarna, County Clare; the place for bachelors and spinsters to seek out a spouse. Much more fun than computer dating.

Cork Film Festival. The popularity of the September festival means that special ferries are run between Britain and the Republic.

Sligo Arts Week.

Waterford Festival of Light Opera.

Ballinasloe October Fair, County Galway, one of Ireland's oldest livestock markets (for cattle and horses).

Dublin Theatre Festival.

Guinness International Jazz Festival, held in Cork and Kinsale.

Kinsale Gourmet Festival. This prestigious festival is the country's best food festival.

Some of the best Kinsale restaurants offer a series of brunches and dinners in the heart of the old fishing village.

Wexford Opera Festival. This 2-week jamboree is Ireland's premier opera event.

The **Dublin Marathon** is usually staged in October.

Waterford Opera Festival. Held in September, this is light opera and less prestigious than the Wexford opera festival, but still good fun.

NOVEMBER – DECEMBER

Start of the hunting, shooting and rugby seasons.

Christmas shopping in Dublin

The Wren Boys, dressed as chimney sweeps with blacked faces, sing and perform in several Irish cities to raise money for charity each year on the 26th of December.

The Royal Dublin Society Summer Festival, at Ballsbridge, Dublin, embraces what was once Ireland's top agricultural show.

Listowel Writers' Week. This fascinating literary festival takes place in County Cork and is a chance to hear Irish writers read their works.

Lough Derg Pilgrimage. From June to mid-August. Pilgrims travel in vast numbers to pray on Holy Island, a monastic site on Lough Derg.

Pilgrimage to the summit of Croagh Patrick, on the last Sunday of the month, in honour of St Patrick.

Puck Fair. Set in Killorglin on the Ring of Kerry, this ancient festival is an excuse for good drinking and carousing in August.

Rose of Tralee. Set in Tralee, this festival is a glorified beauty pageant.

The Dublin Horse Show and Summer Flower Show, the place where the fashionable like to be seen.

Fleadh Ceoil Nan h'Eireann, Sligo, Ireland's premier cultural festival.

Kilkenny Arts Week. A wonderful festival of theatre and music, with events staged in pubs and a variety of small improvised venues all over town.

Practical Information

GETTING THERE

By Air

Dublin airport handles flights from Europe whilst transatlantic flights arrive at Shannon airport. There are frequent flights to both airports and considerable competition between the airlines, including the Irish carriers Aer Lingus and Ryanair. It is well worth shopping around for low-cost fares and fly/drive packages.

Competitive prices are available on all UK-Ireland routes. Virgin (Tel: 0293-747146) offers a smooth flight from London City Airport to Dublin, matched by British Midlands (Tel: 0345-554554) flights from London Heathrow and British Airways (Tel: 0345-222111) flights from London Gatwick. Ryanair (Tel: 071-4357101) offers good economy flights, including from London Stansted. Aer Lingus (Tel: 071-5895599) serves Dublin, Cork, Galway, Kerry, Shannon and Sligo. Its Irish flights connect with Boston, New York, London Heathrow, Manchester, Edinburgh, Paris, Dusseldorf and Frankfurt. Manx Airlines (Tel: 0345-256256) flies from London, Luton to Waterford and the new Kerry Airport, serving Ireland's south east and south west respectively.

From Dublin, the Airlink bus connects with the city centre, bus and rail stations. A taxi to the centre costs £12–15.

By Sea

Two companies offer ferry services from the UK port of Holyhead on the Isle of Anglesea to Dun Laoghaire, just south of Dublin: B&I (Tel: 071-4995744) and Sealink (Tel: 0233-647022). B&I also operates between Pembroke and Rosslare, on the southeast coast, and Sealink sails between Fishguard and Rosslare. Irish Ferries offer three sailings a week between

Going to market

Rosslare and the French ports of Le Havre and Cherbourg (Tel: Rosslare 053-33158 or Dublin 01-6610511).

Travelling to Ireland by ferry is slow (the crossing takes a minimum of 4 hours) and is not necessarily cheaper than flying, though you can take your own car. Again, it is worth shopping around and comparing the costs of a fly/drive package with those of ferry services.

TRAVEL ESSENTIALS

When to Visit

Some of the castles, gardens and museums of most interest to visitors are closed from the end of September through to Easter, so it is best to visit in the main Easter to September season. Gardens and the flora of the Burren are at their best in June, whilst July and August are the busiest months when hotels and restaurants are fullest. Oyster lovers may prefer to visit in September when the new season is celebrated in the Galway area.

Visas and Passports

Passports are required of everyone visiting the Republic except for British citizens. Visas are not required by citizens of European Union member countries, Australia, New Zealand or the USA.

Vaccinations and Health

No vaccinations are required. EU citizens should obtain and file an E111 form to receive free medical care in the event of a problem.

Non-EU citizens are advised to take out health care insurance.

Customs

In addition to the duty-free allowances for cigarettes and alcohol (details are displayed at airports and ferry ports), you can bring in personal possessions without paying duty. It is forbidden to import obscene materials and special rules govern the import of most plant and food products.

Weather

Ireland receives a lot of rain because the prevailing south-westerly winds bring fronts in from the Atlantic. On the other hand the climate is mild, even in winter, because of the effects of the Gulf Stream. Snow covers the higher mountains in winter, but prolonged frost is rare, as can be seen from the many sub-tropical plants that flourish in Ireland.

Clothing

Dublin is both a casual and a formal city. Ladies are extremely smart; gentlemen conflictingly underdressed. For the country, bring comfortable, preferably waterproof, footwear. A strong water-resistant leather shoe or boot is best and Wellington boots are extremely useful.

Ideally clothing should be windproof and waterproof to handle the inevitable showers and the quickly changing weather thrown in from the Atlantic. Sweaters, pullovers and cardigans are a must. Dining at all levels is casual but smart; gentlemen are expected to wear a jacket and tie in top restaurants.

'May the road come up to meet you...'

GETTING ACQUAINTED

Electricity

The standard electric current is 220 Volts, 50 cycles. Most hotels have 110-Volt shaver sockets. Wall sockets are three-pin flat or two-pin round.

Time Difference

Ireland observes Greenwich Mean Time in the winter; from the end of March to the end of September, clocks are one hour ahead of GMT.

Ireland is the most westerly nation in Europe and the island measures 275km (171 miles) at its greatest width and 468km (302 miles) from north to south. The saw-toothed coastline accounts for some 3,173km (1,970 miles) of beaches, inlets, cliffs and coves.

The island consists of an undulating central plain with varying soils, extensively covered with peat bog, a fifth of which is drained by the Shannon river basin. Surrounding the country completely is a broken chain of mountains warmed by the Gulf Stream waters, maintaining a mild and equable climate, normally with a very heavy rainfall.

Government & Economy

The Republic of Ireland enjoys a parliamentary democracy within the EU. The Parliament (*Oireachtas*) consists of the President of the Nation (*Uachtaran na Éireann*) and two houses: an elected House of Representatives (*Dáil Éireann*) and a Senate (*Seanad Éireann*). The president, currently the popular Mary Robinson, is elected by a direct vote of the people for a seven-year term. General elections take place every five years. Elected members of the *Dáil Éireann* use the initials TD after their names.

Ireland's economy depends heavily on trade with other members of the European Union, especially the UK. Agriculture is no longer the most important sector of the economy but still accounts for 10 per cent of the GDP. Ireland has been successful in attracting foreign investment in manufacturing electronics, pharmaceuticals, machinery and transport equipment. Even so, unemployment remains a major problem and the outflow of talented young people from Ireland to the United Kingdom and other European Community countries remains a government concern.

MONEY MATTERS

The monetary unit is the Irish Pound or 'Punt'. Internationally the pound is signified by a prefix of IR£; locally by £, and IEP if written on foreign cheques, including Eurocheques.

Banknotes come in denominations of £1, £5, £10, £20, £50 and £100, but bills above £20 are not advised for casual shopping, only major purchases.

An Irish welcome

Coins come in denominations of £1, 50p, 20p, 10p, 5p, 2p and 1p.

Foreign currencies can be freely changed throughout Ireland in banks and Bureaux de Change. Banking hours generally are Monday to Friday 10am–3pm, many have an hour's lunch-break from 12.30–1.30pm.

Credit cards are accepted all over Ireland in hotels, stores, restaurants and petrol stations.

Tipping

Tipping is not expected in bars. Some hotels and restaurants automatically add a fixed service charge, however.

GETTING AROUND

Driving

For the tours in this guide a car is essential. If you are not bringing your own car over by ferry, you should investigate fly/drive packages offered by the major airlines, or you can rent a car on arrival at Shannon or Dublin airport. Be warned though, car hire is considerably more expensive than in the UK or Continental Europe – however prices vary greatly according to season.

Documents

To drive your own car in Ireland, you need comprehensive insurance valid for Ireland and a driving licence. To rent a car, you need your driving licence and an International Licence.

Rules

Traffic drives on the left. Seat belts must be worn by the driver and front seat passenger. Children must travel in the rear.

Drink driving laws are very strict – it is best not to drink if you intend to drive.

The speed limit on open roads is 90kmh (55mph); in built-up areas it is 65kmh (40mph), in towns and villages 50kmh (30mph).

General

The Republic of Ireland consists of 26 counties and Northern Ireland of six. Most of the higher ground lies close to the coast, while the Midlands tend to be flat, and are often covered by bog. In the west of Ireland, roads tend to be of poorer quality. Travelling Ireland's highways and byways is a joy; traffic is very light in the countryside and drivers are generally careful and courteous.

On country roads, beware of cattle, sheep, dogs, tractors and pedestrians, as well as the occasional pony cart. Many villagers are too poor to own a car and live too remotely for public bus services. It is traditional to offer pedestrians a lift and you can do so with complete safety away from the border.

In the *Gaeltacht* (Irish-speaking areas) many signs will be in Irish only, as is the case on the Dingle Peninsula and in parts of Galway – despite the fact that signs are supposed to be bilingual.

Maps

A good set of maps (such as the Irish Ordnance Survey's 1:250,000 *Holiday Map* series) is essential since it is a national pastime to remove, turn around or even put them upside down!

Healthy living

HOLIDAYS AND HOURS

Shops are generally open 9am–5.30pm Monday to Saturday. Most rural towns have a half-day closing system when shops are shut for one afternoon a week; the day varies from place to place. In cities and larger towns shops stay open until 9pm one day a week – usually on Friday. In Killarney, the tourist capital of Ireland, shops stay open until 10pm in the summer months.

Banks are open 10am–3pm Monday to Friday, though many close between 12.30 and 1.30pm. One afternoon a week (the day varies) they stay open until 5pm.

Bars, pubs and taverns open Monday to Saturday 10.30am–11.30pm and Sunday 12.30–2pm and 4–11pm.

Public holidays are:
1 January
17 March (St Patrick's Day)
Good Friday
Easter Monday
1st Monday in June
1st Monday in August
Last Monday in October
25–26 December

ACCOMMODATION

The ratings used in the guide refer to a double room (with Irish breakfast) in the appropriate price category below:
$$$ = Expensive (£100–250)
$$ = Moderate (£50–100)
$ = Inexpensive (under £50)

Specific recommendations are made at the end of each of our itineraries.

It is advisable to book your accommodation in advance for Dublin, and for all locations between June and the end of September. Reservations can be made through any Bord Fáilte tourist office in Ireland for a small fee to cover telephone costs and a 10 per cent deposit.

Visitors will be inundated with different accommodation guides, all sold at tourist offices and bookshops. The most comprehensive is the Bord Fáilte *Ireland Accommodation Guide* but it concentrates on price not character. Far better are the specific booklets: *Ireland's Blue Guide* (exclusive country house hotels); *The Hidden Ireland* (family-run manors or country houses, all charming); *Farmhouse Accommodation*; *Friendly Homes of Ireland* (family guest houses). In many cases dinner is also offered (with prior notice).

Calling in old bets

EMERGENCIES

For any of the emergency services (police, fire or ambulance) dial 999.

Ireland suffers little of the serious crime that plagues much of the world; even so, you should take precautions to lock and conceal your valuables at all times, and never leave them in a car. In Dublin, especially, use car parks; joyriding and theft from vehicles parked in the streets is all too common. Parking tickets are unusual, except in big cities.

If you need medical or dental services, consult your hotel in the first instance; they will be able to recommend or call out a local doctor/dentist. Medical and dental services are of a very high standard.

EC visitors receive free medical services provided they have completed a form E111; other visitors are advised to get insurance.

COMMUNICATIONS AND NEWS

Post

Postage stamps for mail can be acquired at all post offices, a number of souvenir shops and general convenience stores.

Telephone

Public telephones are plentiful but are mostly card phones so buy an £8 card on arrival. Coin-operated phones accept £1, 50p, 20p, 10p and 5p coins. The minimum charge for a call is 20p.

To dial other countries, first dial the international access code 00, then the country code: Australia (61); France (33); Germany (49); Italy (39); Japan (81); Netherlands (31); Spain (34); UK (44); US and Canada (1). If using a US credit phone card, dial the company's access number below – Sprint, Tel: 1 80055 2001; AT&T, Tel: 1 800 550 000; MCI, Tel: 1 800 551 001. To dial Ireland from overseas, dial 353; for directory enquiries call 190; for international assistance call 114; for the police call 999.

Media

RTE Television offers two channels: RTE1 for current affairs, news and drama; RTE2 for pop. In addition, the British TV networks of BBC1, BBC2, ITV and CHANNEL 4 are available, as are satellite and cable TV.

Ireland has three main newspapers: the *Irish Times* (the best informed), the *Irish Independent* and the *Irish Press*. *In Dublin*, a bi-monthly listings magazine, is worth buying, but also pick up *Tourism News* from tourist offices and the free *Dublin Event Guide* from shopping centres.

LANGUAGE

The language of everyday use is English, even though Gaelic is the official language. English is relatively new, having been forcibly introduced in 1831 to wither Irish national identity.

The revival in Gaelic is due to Eamon de Valera, whose famous quote was 'No language, no country'.

Gaelic is a Celtic language closely related to Breton, Cornish and Welsh with a special alphabet which has distinct and beautiful characters. Today it is fiercely encouraged and taught in schools. Many people in the western areas, known as the Gaeltacht, speak Gaelic as their first tongue and even the road signs are bilingual.

SPORT

Hurling, an ancient game considered to be the fastest field sport in the world, and Gaelic football are played across the whole of Ireland at weekends.

Hurling is played by men (the related game of Camogie is played by women) and is a 15-a-side team game. Players hit a small leather-covered ball with a 'hurley stick', which has a curved blade at its end. Like soccer, the object is to score goals. Gaelic football is also a 15-a-side game best described as a blending of rugby and soccer. Both are exhilarating to play as well as watch.

The 'sport of kings', horse racing, is synonymous with Ireland. Horse racing in Ireland can be traced back to ancient times and wherever you are in Ireland, you are never far away from a county racecourse where you can join in the excitement on a Sunday afternoon.

TOURS

Sections of the itineraries covered in this guide, or in some cases, complete itineraries, can be covered on public transport with careful planning. As a break from driving, consider taking a bus tour.

The Dublin Heritage Bus links many of the sights in Itinerary 1: the Newgrange section of Itinerary 2 can be covered on a Greylines Tour (booked through Dublin tourist office); Itinerary 3 can also be done as an organised excursion from Dublin. Itinerary 16 (Kilkenny and Rock of Cashel) is visited by organised tours from Dublin or Waterford.

The west and the south west are well-covered by tours that cover or overlap itineraries 7, 8, 11, 12, 13 and 14. Such organised tours are available from Cork, Galway, Killarney and Tralee tourist offices. Also call Bus Eirann (Tel: 012-508188). Most tours only run in summer, but in Killarney, Dero's also runs tours out of season (Tel: 064-31251).

USEFUL ADDRESSES

Tourist offices

The Irish Tourist Board (Bord Fáilte), has offices in most towns. They exist not just to supply information but also to act as travel agents; you can use them to book accommodation, sightseeing tours, car rental, flights and ferries, theatre tickets and so on.

They will also supply information on sport, diving, golf, cycling, fishing and any other type of special interest activity. Finally, all have a Bureau de Change and a shop selling maps, books and quality handicrafts.

A complete list of all offices is available from any Bord Fáilte office in Ireland or worldwide.

The following regional offices are open all year round:

Adare	061-396255
Cork	021-273251
Dingle	066-51241
Dublin Airport	01-8445387
Dublin City	01-8747733
Ennis	065-28366
Galway	091-63081
Kilkenny	056-21755
Killarney	064-31633
Kinsale	021-772234
Letterkenny	074-21160
Limerick	061-317522
Monaghan	047-81122
Shannon Airport	061-471664
Skibbereen	028-21766
Sligo	071-61201
Tralee	066-21288
Waterford	051-75788
Westport	098-25711
Wexford	053-23111

FURTHER READING

Beckett, J C. *The Making of Modern Ireland*. Faber.
Bell, Brian (ed). *Insight Guide: Ireland*, and *Insight Cityguide Dublin*. Apa Publications.
Doyle, Roddy. *Dublin Trilogy*.
Delany, Frank. *James Joyce's Odyssey – A Guide to the Dublin of Ulysses*. Hodder & Stoughton.
Fitzgibbon, Theodora. *A Taste of Ireland*. Pan.
Gogarty, Oliver St John. *As I Was Going Down Sackville Street*. Sphere.
Harbison, Peter. *Guide to National and Historic Monuments in Ireland*. Gill and Macmillan.
Joyce, James. *Ulysses* and *Dubliners*.
Jeffares and Kamm (eds). *Irish Childhoods* (*an anthology*). Gill and Macmillan.
Kee, Robert. *Ireland – A History*. Weidenfeld.
Kinsella, Thomas. *The New Oxford Book of Irish Verse*. OUP.
Keneally, Thomas. *Now and In the Time to Be*. Flamingo.
McKenna, John and Sally. *The Bridgestone Irish Food Guide*. Estragon Press.
Murphy, Dervla, *Ireland*. Salem House.
O'Faolain Sean. *The Irish: A Character Study*. Penguin Books.
Pritchett, V S. *Dublin, A Portrait*. Harper Row.
Somerville-Large, Peter. *Dublin*. Hamish Hamilton and *The Coast of West Cork*. Appletree. Hamilton.

Index

A

Abbeyfeale 59
Achill Head 45
Adare (Ath Dara) 58
Adare Manor 55
Aghadoe 63
Ahenny 75
Aillwee Caves 52
Annascaul 61
Anne's Grove 72
Ardagh 58
Ardagh Chalice, The 11, 24, 58
Ardara 84
Arthurstown 78
Aughnanure Castle 46

B

Balbriggan 29
Ballintaggart 61
Ballyferriter 62
Ballyhack 79
Ballyshannon 36
Baltimore 66
Bantry 13, 66
Battle of the Boyne 13
Bective Abbey 31
Benbulben 37-8
Blarney Castle 68-9
Blasket Islands 62
Blennerville 60
Blessington 34
Blessington Lakes 34
'Book of Kells' 11, 23
Brendan Boat 56
Bridgetown Abbey 73
Bundoran 37
Bunratty 56
Burren, The 52, 93
Burrishoole Abbey 44

C

Cahir 75-6
Camp 60
Cappoquin 74
Carrick on Suir 75
Carrowmore 40
Cashel 49
Castle Matrix 58
Castleisland 59
Castletown 13
Castletownroche 72
Castletownshend 67
Charles Fort 69
Christchurch Cathedral 21, 25
Church of St Nicholas (Galway) 49
Clare Island 43
Clarinbridge 51
Cleggan 48
Clew Bay 44
Clifden 48
Cliffs of Moher 54
Clonmel 75
Clonmines 79
Cobh 70
Connacht 10, 40, 48
Connor Pass 62
Cork 69-70, 72
Cormac's Chapel 76
Crag Cave 59
Craggaunowen Project 56
Creevykeel Court Cairn 37
Croagh Patrick 43, 91
Curraun Peninsula 44

D, E

Deerpark (megalithic complex) 40
Dingle 61
Dominican Abbey (Sligo) 39
Donegal town 35

100

Dooagh 44
Dooega (Dumha Eige) 44
Dowth 10, 31
Drogheda 29
Drombeg 67
Drumcliffe 37
Dublin 20-6
Dugort 45
Dunbeg 61
Dungaire Castle 51-2
Ennis 54
Ennistymon 54

F, G

Fahan 61
Falls of Donermarc 65
Fermoy 73
Fethard 79
Folk Park (Bunratty) 56
Fota Estate 70
Four Courts 13, 26
Foynes 58
Gallarus Oratory 62
Galway 46, 49
Garinish Island 65
Glandore 67
Glanworth 73
Glencar Lough 39
Glendalough 33
Glengarriff 65
Glin (An Gleann) 59
GPA Aviation Museum 58
Grange 37
Guinness Brewery 26

H

Harvey's Point 36, 38
Hazelwood 40
Hill O'Doon 46
Hill of Slane 31
Hook Head 79
Hotels
  Adare 55
  Bantry 65
  Clifden 50
  Cork 70
  Donegal 38
  Dublin 28
  Galway 50
  Kilkenny 77
  Kinsale 68
  Limerick 55

Newmarket-on-Fergus 55
Sligo 38
Tralee 60
Waterford 74
Westport 45
Hunt Collection 57

I, J

Ilnacullin 65
Inch 60
Inishbofin Island 48
Innisfree (lake isle of) 39
Innishmurray Island 37
Irish National Heritage Park 80
Jerpoint Abbey 77
Johnstown Castle 80
Joyce Museum 32

K

Keel 44
Keem Strand 44
Kells (County Kilkenny) 77
Kells (County Meath) 12
Kenmare 65
Kilbarron Castle 36
Kildownet Castle 44
Kilfenora 53
Kilkenny 12, 76
Kilkieran (CillCiaráin) 49
Killarney 63-4
Killary Harbour 43
Kilmalkedar Church 62
Kilmore 79
King John's Castle 56, 57
Kinsale 68
Knocknarea 40
Knowth 10, 31
Kylemore Abbey 47

L, M

Labbacallee wedge tomb 73
Leamaneh Castle 53
Leenane 44
Leinster 10
Leinster House 13, 24
Letterfrack 47
Limerick 55–9
Lisdoonvarna 53, 92
Lismore 73
Lissadell House 37
Listowel 59

Louisburg 43
Lusk 29
Maam Cross 46
Malahide Castle 29
Mallow Castle 72
Mansion House 24
Mellifont Abbey 30
Monasterboice 30
Muckross Abbey 64
Muckross House 64
Mullaghmore 37
Mulrany (Mallaranny) 44
Munster 10

N–Q

National Gallery of Ireland 21
National Gallery's portrait collection 23
National Museum 11, 24
Natural History Museum 24
Navan 31
Newbridge House 13
Newgrange 10, 30-1
Newman House 24
Newport 44
Old Head of Kinsale 67
Oughterard 46
Parkes Castle 40
Piper Stones 34
Poulnabrone Dolmen 53
Powerscourt 13, 33
Powerscourt Townhouse complex 82
Queenstown Story, Cobh 70
Quin 56

R

Rathkeale (Ráth Caola) 58
Rathmacknee Castle 80
Reask 62
Restaurants (cf *Eating Out* section)
  Adare 55
  Bantry 65
  Clarinbridge 55
  Clifden 50
  Cork 70
  Donegal 38
  Dublin 27-28
  Galway 50
  Kilkenny 77
  Kinsale 68
  Limerick 55
  Tralee 60

Waterford 74
Westport 45
Roche Castle 73
Rock of Cashel 75
Roonah Quay 43
Rosses Point 39
Rothe House 76
Roundstone 48
Royal Irish Academy Library 24
Russborough House 13, 34

S

St Anne's Church (Dublin) 24
St Canice's Cathedral 77
St Colman's Cathedral 70
St Finbar's Cathedral 69
St Michan's Church (Dublin) 26
St Muiredach Cross 30
St Multose Church 68
St Patrick 17, 24, 31, 91
St Patrick's Cathedral 17, 24
St Peter's Church (Drogheda) 30
St Stephen's Green 24
Sally Gap 34
Saltee Islands 79
Sandycove 32
Seven Sisters stones 64
Shee Almshouse 76
Sheep's Head Peninsula 66
Skerries 29
Skibbereen 66
Slade 79
Slane 31
Slea Head 61-2
Sligo town 39
Sraith Salach (Recess) 47
Swiss Valley 39
Swords 29

T, V

Tara Brooch 11, 24, 58
Tarbert 59
Teampall Lobhair 73
Temple Bar 26
Timoleague Abbey 67
Tintern Abbey 79
Torc Waterfall 64
Tralee 60
Tramore 74
Trim 32
Trinity College 21

V, W, Y

Ventry 61
Waterford 74, 75, 77, 78–9
Westport 42–3
Wexford 80
Wicklow Mountains 34
Wildfowl Protection Area (North Slob) 80
Wood Quay 26
Yeats, William Butler (grave of) 37, 38
Youghal 74

Acknowledgments

Photography	**Guy Mansell** *and*
Pages 14–15, 24, 59, 74, 75, 76–7T, 77B, 80, 83, 85,	**Bord Fáilte**
20	**Phil Crean**
56	**Shannon Dev**
91	**Barry Lewis**
11T, 23T, 44, 45B, 48B, 49, 54, 67T, 84, 87, 92	**Brian Lynch**
8/9, 87	**Antonio Martinelli**
62B	**Office of Public Works**
16	**Pat O'Dea**
27	**G P Reichelt**
2/3	**Tony Stone Worldwide**
76B	**Tipperary Crystal**
Cover Design	**Klaus Geisler**
Cartography	**Berndtson & Berndtson**
Layout/Production	**Mohammed Dar**

The editors would like to thank Mr John Lahiffe of the Irish Tourist Board in London for his help with arcane spellings and photographs of obscure sites, and Miss Caroline McEldowney and family for their timely assistance gathering *objets trouvés*.